OSPREY MILITARY CAMPAIGN S

MAJUBA 1881

THE HILL OF DESTINY

SERIES EDITOR: LEE JOHNSON

OSPREY MILITARY CAMPAIGN SERIES: 45

MAJUBA 1881

THE HILL OF DESTINY

IAN CASTLE

First published in Great Britain in 1996 by OSPREY, a division of Reed Consumer Books Limited, Michelin House, 81 Fulham Road, London SW3 6RB and Auckland, Melbourne, Singapore and Toronto

ISBN 1 85532 503 9

Military Editor: Sharon van der Merwe
Designed by TT Designs

Colour bird's eye view illustrations by Peter Harper.
Cartography by Micromap.
Battle scene artwork by Dawn Waring
Wargaming Majuba by Richard Brooks.

Filmset in Great Britain.
Printed through World Print Ltd., Hong Kong

For a catalogue of all books published by Osprey Military please write to:

The Marketing Manager, Consumer Catalogue Department, Osprey Publishing Ltd., Michelin House, 81 Fulham Road, London SW3 6RB

Acknowledgements

The author would like to express his gratitude to Ian Knight, Rai England, Michael Barthop and Lt.-Col. Ian Bennett for their generous help in the preparation of this book.

Except where specified, illustrations are from the Author's collection.

KEY TO MILITARY SERIES SYMBOLS

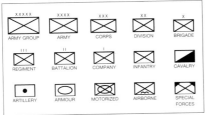

PAGE 2 **The rout at Majuba. Those British who were not injured as they careered down the mountain became easy targets for the Boers lining the edge of the mountain, who likened it to shooting game.**

PAGE 3 **The Boers brought much fire to bear on the artillery at Schuinshoogte, since the gunners presented clear targets while loading and firing their pieces, and half their men were hit. The small inset shows Colley's miraculous night escape across the flooded Ingogo River.**

CONTENTS

THE ROAD TO WAR 1881

In 1881 the British Empire embarked on another of the 'little wars' that had become commonplace for the Victorian Army in the latter half of the 19th century. However, this time there were to be no glorious battle honours added to the annals of the Army; only defeat and humiliation. Depending on your viewpoint at the time, the conflict was known as either the Transvaal Rebellion or the Transvaal War of Independence. Today it is more generally known as the First Anglo-Boer War. Regardless of its name, it was to leave the British Army frustrated and burning with a desire for revenge.

The roots of the conflict lay 50 years earlier in the Great Trek, the mass exodus of Dutch-speaking settlers from the Cape Colony. Their purpose was to find a new land for themselves in the interior of Africa, far from the constraints and interference of the British Colonial authorities, where they could continue their traditional pastoral way of life. These people, the Boers, favoured an independent and solitary life, guided by a strict religious code. Their lifestyle had been dramatically affected by the arrival of the British in southern Africa.

A panoramic view of the theatre of operations from the heliograph station on Signal Hill, just north of Newcastle:
1. Schuinshoogte. 2. Majuba. 3. Mount Prospect Camp. 4. Laing's Nek. (I. Knight)

BRITAIN TAKES CONTROL OF THE CAPE OF GOOD HOPE

As a result of the Napoleonic Wars, Britain had officially gained ownership of the Cape of Good Hope in 1814, although they had occupied it since 1806. This removed the Boers from Dutch influence and placed them under British rule and subject to British laws. In addition, the Boers' strict religious beliefs, which had imbued in them the conviction that they were infinitely superior to the indigenous black inhabitants of the land they now occupied, were being threatened. Matters came to a head in 1834, when Britain ordered the emancipation of all slaves throughout the Empire. The government's inadequate system for reimbursement, combined with an equalling of the status of black and white in law, convinced the Boers that the time had come to seek a new homeland.

The Great Trek

The Great Trek that followed took the Boers northwards and across the Orange river. Some settled there; others veered to the east, crossed the Drakensberg mountains and entered Natal, while still more pushed further north, across the Vaal river. Unhappy with the emigration of some 12,000 of her subjects, Britain passed an Act which extended the jurisdiction of its law well beyond the Vaal.

Unable to shake off what they considered foreign involvement in their lives, the Boers clashed with the British at Port Natal (Durban) in 1842 and at Zwartkopjes in 1845. In 1848 Britain annexed the whole area between the Orange and Vaal rivers, which resulted in a further clash, at Boomplaats. The Boers were defeated each time.

However, the increasing expense of maintaining these new far-flung corners of the Empire prompted a change in attitude, which resulted in the Sand River Convention, signed in 1852. This offered the Boers beyond the Vaal what they had long awaited: freedom from British rule. The Transvaal was officially named the South African Republic, and two years later it was joined in independence by the neighbouring Orange Free State.

Britain was happy to leave these fledgling republics to their own devices, but the discovery of diamonds in the area in the late 1860s reawakened her interest and that of all parties in the area. Claims to ownership were made by local Griquas, the Orange Free State and the Transvaal. Arbitration settled the dispute in favour of the Griquas; Britain then announced that the area, Griqualand West, was to become a British dependency. Anti-British feelings were running high in the Orange Free State and even more so in the Transvaal, where the president was forced to resign. His replacement, Thomas Burgers, although determined to develop various progressive ideas, was severely hampered by the extreme difficulty in extracting taxes from the staunchly individualistic population.

The potential mineral wealth that southern Africa could contribute to the Imperial coffers changed Britain's attitude to an area which had previously been considered a drain on resources. If this situation was to be exploited fully, something would have to be done to straighten out the tangle of British colonies, Boer republics and independent African

kingdoms that populated this land. Lord Carnarvon, the Colonial Secretary in London, began planning a policy of Confederation which would bring all these separate lands together under British control enabling economic growth to flourish.

In April 1877 the British government annexed the bankrupt Transvaal and hoisted the British flag in Pretoria. This photograph was taken one month later at the Queen's birthday celebrations in the military camp. (I. Knight)

ANNEXATION OF THE TRANSVAAL

Events in the Transvaal now began to favour those planning confederation. In 1876 the Boers fought an unsuccessful war against the Pedi king, Sekhukhune. The cost to the Transvaal government was high, forcing President Burgers to levy a war tax of £5 on every burgher. Most refused to pay, and the national debt reached £215,000. It was reported that the treasury contained only 12 shillings and sixpence. The Transvaal, surrounded by potentially hostile black neighbours, found itself bankrupt and dangerously exposed.

Taking advantage of this situation the British government appointed Sir Theophilus Shepstone as Special Commissioner to the South African Republic, with instructions to annex the country. With the support of the mainly British population around Pretoria, Shepstone hoisted the Union Flag over the capital on 12 April 1877. There was no protest. President Burghers was retired on a pension and instructed to leave the Transvaal.

At the annexation ceremony Shepstone, now the Transvaal Administrator, made a number of promises regarding the future development of the country. As these promises failed to materialise, the Boers

RIGHT **Potchefstroom. On 11 November 1880 Bezuidenhout's wagon was due to be auctioned here, but it was forcibly removed by a group of Boers. A month later the first shots of the war were exchanged in the town. (R. England)**

became more suspicious and sullen over British rule. Protests grew, and two deputations were sent to London in an attempt to reverse the annexation. These protests were largely ignored, but led to the recall of Shepstone in 1879. His replacement was Colonel Owen Lanyon, whose overbearing military manners and arrogant attitude soon earned him the hatred of all Boers who came into contact with him.

In January 1879 Britain went to war against the Zulu kingdom. The roots of the war lay in the policy of confederation. The annexation of the Transvaal had brought with it a long-running boundary dispute between the Transvaal Boers and the Zulus. Sir Bartle Frere, the High Commissioner for southern Africa, used the settlement of this dispute to issue an ultimatum to the Zulus which spelt war. With the defeat of the Zulus another piece could be placed in the confederation jigsaw. Frere had expected the Boers to join the invading army, but only a few volunteered; many others hoped for a British defeat.

The removal of the powerful Zulu threat from the border, through eventual defeat at Ulundi in July 1879, brought a new confidence to the Transvaal Boers. Sir Garnet Wolseley, who by now was High Commissioner for Natal, Zululand and the Transvaal, continued talks with the Boers, but his firm, inflexible stance irritated them. Wolseley's position was epitomised by his statement: 'So long as the sun shines, the Transvaal will remain British territory.'

The Boers aired their grievances at mass meetings in the country and many thousands would attend. Tax was a favourite topic at these meetings. Lanyon had set to with a single-minded determination to

ABOVE **Piet Bezuidenhout, the spark that lit the fire. Summonsed for tax arrears, he proved the authorities wrong, but when he refused to pay costs the authorities seized his wagon to settle the debt.** (National Army Museum)

redress the shortfall of taxes over the previous years, although there were no records of who had or had not paid what was due. To solve this problematical situation it was decided to impose an estimated arrears where there was some doubt if taxes had been paid. It would then become the responsibility of the defendant to prove that the estimate was incorrect rather than the government to prove otherwise. Needless to say, the Boers were incensed, but the Treasury grew.

In April 1880 Wolseley returned to Britain, firmly believing that the Transvaal was about to enter a new peaceful phase. He had misjudged the situation. The Boers had become less vociferous for a reason. In Britain an election was imminent in which Gladstone's Liberals were expected to come to power; Gladstone had spoken out against the annexation and in favour of Boer independence. In April 1880 the Liberals did indeed come to power, but they immediately became embroiled in more pressing problems and refused to honour their promises to the Transvaal.

Wolseley's replacement was Sir George Pomeroy-Colley, but he was instructed to avoid involvement in the Transvaal unless it proved absolutely necessary. Lanyon, now Sir Owen, was made Governor of the Transvaal, over the people who disliked him so much.

THE OUTBREAK OF WAR

In November 1880 a Boer named Piet Bezuidenhout was summoned to appear before the *landdrost* (magistrate) of Potchefstroom for tax arrears. Bezuidenhout was ordered to pay arrears of £27 5s but was able to prove that he only owed £14. The *landdrost* consulted with Pretoria and was instructed to accept the £14 but charge Bezuidenhout costs, which brought the total claim back to £27 5s. He refused to pay costs to correct a mistake made by the government, so the *landdrost* seized his wagon and prepared to offer it at a public sale to settle the debt. On the appointed day a body of about 100 armed Boers rode into Potchefstroom, forcibly took possession of the wagon and removed it. Lanyon ordered a military force to march to Potchefstroom to support the civil authority there, but informed London that he did not anticipate that 'any serious trouble' would arise out of the affair.

In light of these developments the Boers brought forward their next planned mass meeting from January to December. Lanyon declared the meeting illegal, but some 4,000 Boers congregated at a farm known as Paardekraal. They voted overwhelmingly to demand the restoration of the South African Republic, by force of arms if necessary. A Triumvirate – Paul Kruger, Piet Joubert and Marthinus Pretorious – was elected to organise a government. The Triumvirate moved to Heidelberg to set up a provisional capital while a large body of mounted men were despatched to Potchefstroom to arrange for the printing of their demand for the restoration of the Republic. The troops which Lanyon had ordered to the town were now in position in a small earthwork fort. Outnumbered by the Boers, who took over the town, the British attempted to negotiate, but tension increased. Insults were exchanged between the soldiers in the fort and the Boers in the town, a shot rang out and was returned; war had begun.

OPPOSING COMMANDERS

MAJOR-GENERAL
SIR GEORGE POMEROY-COLLEY,
KCSI, CB, CMG

Sir George Colley arrived in Durban in July 1880 to take up his new appointment as Her Majesty's High Commissioner for South-Eastern Africa, Governor of Natal, and Commander-in-Chief of all British troops in the Transvaal and Natal. Colley's abilities had been well noted for some time, and as one of Sir Garnet Wolseley's favoured circle of officers he was marked for a long and glittering career.

Born in 1835 into an Anglo-Irish family, Colley entered the Royal Military College at Sandhurst at the age of 13. In 1852 he joined the 2nd Regiment of Foot as an ensign, and became a lieutenant in 1854. He then travelled to southern Africa to take up a post as a border magistrate, a position he held for five years. In 1860 he rejoined his regiment and took part in the war in China before returning to Africa as a captain.

Colley's star was now in its ascendancy, and in 1862 he left Africa to enter the Staff College. There his aptitude for military theory came to the fore, and in nine months he completed the two-year course and achieved the highest marks that had been awarded up to that time. Now a major, a post as army examiner at Sandhurst followed before he became Professor of Military Administration.

In 1873 the prospect of war in the West African kingdom of Asante led to the appointment of Sir Garnet Wolseley as commander of a force detailed to defeat the army of King Kofi Karikari. Wolseley personally selected the officers who would form his staff. Colley was included in this number and was handed responsibility for the transport affairs of the column. He applied himself vigorously to the task and successfully brought order to a chaotic situation. This earned him generous praise from Wolseley, and Colley was promoted to full colonel and made a Companion of the Bath.

Wolseley was appointed Governor of Natal in 1875 and took Colley with him as a member of his staff. A year later Colley left to become private secretary to the Viceroy of India, but when Wolseley was recalled to Natal during the Zulu War of 1879, Colley rejoined him there as Chief of Staff. With the successful conclusion of the war, Colley returned to India, but in 1880, following the forceful recommendation of Wolseley, he journeyed back to Africa once more, this time taking his position as the supreme civil and military authority in Natal and the Transvaal.

For the first time Colley was in sole command, with no illustrious superiors to rely upon. Although now a major-general, he had never held any individual military command and lacked practical experience. However, Sir Evelyn Wood regarded Colley as 'the best instructed soldier I ever met'.

Colley was a kind and sensitive man. He had the bearing of a gentleman, was modest yet suffered from shyness and self-doubt. The Boers hoped for an improvement in relations, since Colley appeared more approachable than either Wolseley or Lanyon, but they were to be disappointed. Colley had been instructed to avoid involvement in the Transvaal if possible and accordingly he accepted Lanyon's optimistic appraisals of the situation uncritically.

Unfortunately for Colley, his years of service in southern Africa meant that he already held an opinion of the Boers as a people and of their disposition and resilience. In 1875 he had accompanied a Boer commando on a diplomatic mission to Swaziland. He had labelled the Boers an 'undisciplined rabble' and concluded that they would be unable to stand and face a regular force. This opinion had received added strength from the Boers' poor performance against Sekhukhune in 1876. Following a tour of the Transvaal in August 1880, Colley saw nothing to change his opinion and he was further reassured by reports which informed him that the Boers were beginning to tire of the agitation that had been prevalent for so long. Indeed, as late as 5 December 1880, Lanyon, the man on the spot in the Transvaal, was advising that there was little cause for anxiety. When the startling news of the ambush of a detachment of the 94th Regiment at Bronkhorstspruit reached Colley on Christmas Day 1880, he was rudely made aware of the Boers' determination to fight for their freedom.

Sir George Pomeroy-Colley. After passing brilliantly through staff college he became an examiner at Sandhurst before duties in West Africa, Natal and India. He returned to southern Africa in 1880 and succeeded Wolseley as supreme civil and military authority.

COMMANDANT-GENERAL PETRUS JACOBUS JOUBERT

Joubert was born in 1831, a descendant of French Huguenots who had come to southern Africa in the late 17th century. He was elected Commandant-General of the Transvaal Republican forces at the mass meeting at Paardekraal in December 1880, although he claimed that he lacked the required talent for the task ahead.

When Joubert was six years old his parents had joined the Great Trek and settled in Natal. Later he moved to the Transvaal, settling in the Wakkerstroom district, close to the future theatre of war. Joubert succeeded in educating himself and developed a strong interest in law, which enabled him to come to the fore as a politician. In 1873 he became Chairman of the *Volksraad* (parliament) and was Vice-President of the Republic until he resigned from the position.

He returned to the political scene following the annexation of the Republic in 1877. He visited Britain in 1878 with Kruger as part of a deputation seeking to restore the former independence of the Transvaal but was unsuccessful. Joubert and Kruger did not always see eye to eye, but Joubert was always careful to keep on good terms with people whenever possible. A tall and powerful man, Joubert spoke English well, and was known as 'Slim Piet' by his followers, *slim* being a Boer word describing guile and craftiness. He had a fiery spirit and was well respected for his generosity and, like Colley, his kindness.

Second in command to Joubert, and ideally suitable for this job, was Commandant Nicholas Smit, a man in his mid-forties. Although a farmer, like the majority of the Boers, he had an unrivalled natural talent for military matters. His effective use of cover was second to none, and Colley himself commented early in the war that Smit was 'an intelligent and fine man, courteous and humane in everything connected with the wounded, and gallant in action'. Together, Joubert and Smit were about to shock and silence the British military, who had repeatedly derided and taunted the Boers as cowards.

ABOVE **Petrus (Piet) Joubert had stepped down from political life but was drawn back by the annexation. He was elected to the Triumvirate and became commander of the armed forces of the Transvaal Republic in December 1880.**
(National Army Museum)

LEFT **Nicholas Smit was second in command to Joubert and, although a farmer, proved to be a natural soldier. He was described as one of the ablest leaders of mounted infantry of his time.**
(National Army Museum)

OPPOSING ARMIES

BRITISH ARMY

At the conclusion of the Zulu War in July 1879 15 regular infantry battalions and two cavalry regiments available for service in Natal and Zululand. On the eve of war, 17 months later, this number had dwindled to four battalions distributed throughout Natal and the Transvaal and no cavalry support. The six 9-pdr RML guns of N Battery, 5th Brigade, Royal Artillery were also available, but these too were distributed, four in the Transvaal and two in Natal.

The four imperial battalions were: 2nd Battalion 21st Regiment; 58th Regiment; 3rd Battalion, 60th Rifles; and 94th Regiment. All four had fought in the latter stages of the Zulu War, and both the 2/21st and the 94th regiments had taken part in the second campaign against Sekhukhune, late in 1879. However, for the rest of their posting in Africa the tedious periods of garrison duty in isolated posts which followed had had a bad effect on morale, and cases of desertion had been increasing.

The line infantry regiments were still equipped as they had been during the Zulu War. Scarlet tunics (either the dress tunic or undress serge frock) were worn with the regimental colour displayed on a small tab at the front of the collar and on a cuff patch. The regiment's number was displayed on the shoulder strap and a badge was worn on the coloured collar tab. Dark blue trousers with a red welt down the outside seam completed the basic uniform. The exception to this was the 3/60th. As a rifle regiment they wore dark green (almost black) uniforms with black leather equipment replacing the buff leather type used by line regiments. (For more details see Osprey: Elite 32 *British Forces in Zululand 1879*).

At the outbreak of war British line regiments were still wearing their traditional, highly visible, scarlet tunics. This photo shows men of the 2/21st at Fort Commeline outside Pretoria during the war. (Local History Museum, Durban)

Headwear was the white foreign service helmet, but this had proved highly conspicuous during the Zulu War, and the practice of dying the helmet to give it a more natural look continued throughout the war with the Transvaal. The standard infantry weapon was the single-shot breech-loading Mark II Martini-Henry rifle, which had proved effective against the Zulus in 1879.

To supplement this meagre force and cover his deficiency in cavalry, Colley organised a scratch mounted squadron. The core of this unit was to be 35 dismounted members of the 1st King's Dragoon Guard, who were awaiting transport back to England. They were joined by 25 members of No.7 Company, Army Service Corps and 60 men drawn from the 58th Regiment and 3/60th. The men were quickly given mounts, and this unlikely combination was sent off to the front. In addition 70 men of the quasi-military Natal Mounted Police were placed under Colley's command.

When it became obvious that war was unavoidable, efforts were made to improve the quantity of artillery available. Two 9-pdrs were released from stores in Natal and 10/7 Battery sent some men from garrison duty in Cape Town to man them. Additionally, two 7-pdr guns were also discovered in stores, but in the absence of any artillerymen to man them, volunteers were drawn from the 3/60th.

The above image of the smart British soldier soon disappeared once on campaign. Taking the 94th Regiment as an example of a typical unit, they had embarked from England in February 1879, and had worn the same tunics and trousers from then right through the Zulu War and the campaign against Sekhukhune. It seems that new tunics and trousers were received sometime in 1880, but a description by Brevet Lieutenant-Colonel Philip Anstruther, 94th Regiment, of his men prior to the arrival of this consignment conjures up a vivid picture of a regiment in the field: 'Their coats and trousers are all colours –cords, blue serge, red ditto, any mufti they can lay their hands on patched all over with sacking, skin or anything.' It seems that their equipment also suffered from fatigue, and helmets had not been replaced prior to the outbreak of war. The white helmets that had looked so pristine and smart when the 94th left England were now hardly recognisable as headwear. Some crumpled examples survived, but many men wore anything they could buy, find or make from skins.

LEFT **Uniformed in scarlet tunics and dark blue trousers with a wide yellow stripe, the King's Dragoon Guards formed the core of the Mounted Squadron. They were joined by volunteers from the Army Service Corps, 58th and 3/60th.**

Even with this limited force, Colley felt more than able to control any aggressive moves by the Boers in the Transvaal. He had long held a belief in the ability of small bodies of British troops to achieve much, but there were those who were concerned that Colley held a 'dangerously high idea of what a few British soldiers can do'.

THE TRANSVAAL REPUBLICAN ARMY

The term 'army' is not entirely correct. The Boer forces were in fact an armed citizen militia. The commando system they employed had come into being during the early 18th century, providing an ideal response to the raiding nature of the indigenous population of the exposed frontier areas. Prior to the outbreak of war the Transvaal had been divided into 12 electoral districts, each of which was required to provide a mounted commando, under a commandant, within 48 hours of the announcement of mobilisation. The responsibility to bring the men together fell to the *veld kornets* (field cornets)– two or three elected men from each district. All able-bodied men between 16 and 60 were obliged to turn out, equipping themselves with horse, saddlery, rifle, cartridges and eight days' rations. There was no pay for being on commando; it was considered a necessary collective civil responsibility. In theory the Transvaal could muster about 7,000 men in this way. The prospect of a forthcoming war meant that the limited amount of ammunition available in the Transvaal was a concern. However, this was overcome when an arsenal was created at Heidelberg after the declaration of independence, and this soon began to produce 2,500 cartridges per day.

When the Boer went to war, he armed himself not only with a rifle but also with the ballot. Each man was an individual and expected to be treated as such. On campaign regular councils of war were held, during which matters of strategy and tactics were openly discussed and decisions voted on by all present.

The appearance of the Boer was derided by the British, who often regarded their future enemies as comical, country-bumpkin types. One officer described a typical Boer as 'a dirty unkempt-looking fellow, with long hair and beard, very much tanned, his face the colour of mahogany,

The Boers were derided by British officers for their appearance. They were considered comical, unkempt and unsoldierly, and their mastery of horse and gun was largely ignored – with tragic consequences. (R. England)

The Boers favoured a defensive strategy, refusing to expose themselves recklessly to enemy fire. If an enemy closed, they would quickly remount and retire to the next suitable position. (R. England)

a generally broad-shouldered, hard-looking man, his dress of all sorts and conditions – usually a coat that will just hold together, and a pair of baggy corduroy trousers. The chances are he had one spur on upside down, his head covered with a broad-brimmed felt hat, high in the crown, and a dirty flannel shirt'. But despite their appearance, the Boer was both an expert rider and marksman. A lifetime in the saddle had taught respect for his steed, while an inbred need to defend and provide for his family ensured that the Boer rarely wasted his precious ammunition.

The Boers favoured a defensive strategy; they were not soldiers and saw little purpose in exposing themselves to enemy fire if avoidable. To this end a Boer would happily hold a secure defensive position until such time as it appeared the enemy were about to close. At this point he would mount his horse (hidden in dead ground nearby) and retire to safety or to a new vantage point and live to fight again. The rules and etiquette of European warfare were little known or respected by the Boer.

The Boers had a wide range of firearms available to them. As the gun was so important to their lifestyle, every man would try to acquire the very best weapon he could. Of the many types available, perhaps the most popular was the Westley Richards falling block, single action, breech-loading rifle. A good weapon such as this in the hands of an excellent marksman could prove a lethal combination.

OPPOSING PLANS

THE BRITISH POSITION

The Boers' declaration of independence at Paardekraal in December 1880 and the subsequent firing of shots at Potchefstroom stunned the British authorities. Throughout the period of Britain's annexation it had always been felt that the Boers would eventually tire of negotiations and accept their place within the British Empire. No-one really believed that the Boers would be prepared to fight for their independence. These first few shots now exposed the weakness of the British position in the Transvaal.

Pretoria, with a small garrison of regulars, was the headquarters for the British in the Transvaal, but many of the available troops were stationed in isolated encampments across the region. These detachments were spread too far apart to be able to offer support to one another. At the beginning of November their distribution was as follows:

Pretoria	HQ, 5 coys. and mounted troop of 2/21st Regiment, 4 9-pdrs of N/5 Battery, about 45 Royal Engineers and some Army Service Corps and Army Hospital Corps personnel.
Rustenburg	2 coys. 2/21st Regiment.
Lydenburg	HQ and 2 coys. 94th Regiment.
Marabastad	2 coys. 94th Regiment.
Wakkerstroom	1 coy. and mounted troop of 94th Regiment.
Standerton	1 coy. 94th Regiment.

Following the Bezuidenhout incident in Potchefstroom, one company and the mounted troop of the 2/21st, stationed in Pretoria, were despatched there with two of the 9-pdrs. One company of 2/21st based in Rustenburg was also sent there. These men were sent purely to bolster the civil officials, but they formed the garrison when the first shots were fired, on 16 December 1880. The commander of the British troops in the Transvaal, Colonel Bellairs, had not felt quite so complacent about

THEATRE OF OPERATIONS AND BESIEGED GARRISONS: DECEMBER 1880-MARCH 1881

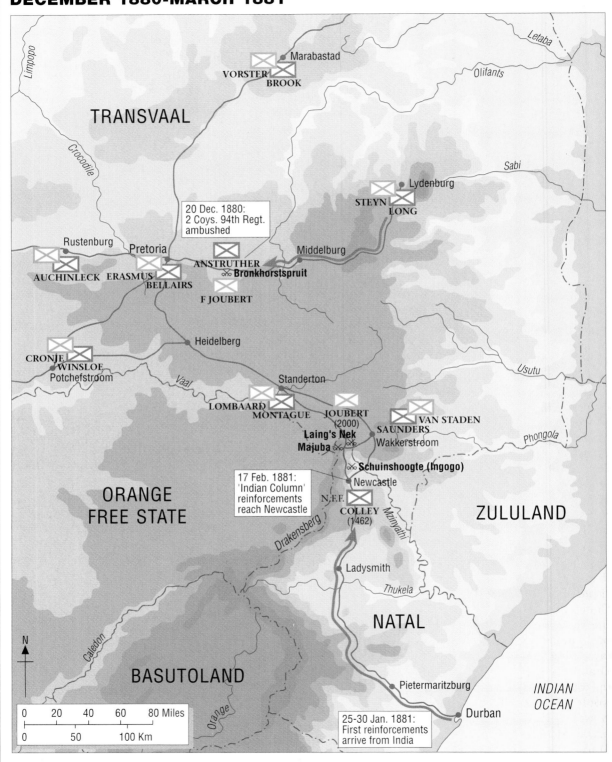

Letaba

Limpopo

Olifants

TRANSVAAL

Crocodile

Sabi

VORSTER
BROOK
Marabastad

STEYN
LONG
Lydenburg

20 Dec. 1880:
2 Coys. 94th Regt.
ambushed

Rustenburg

Pretoria

Middelburg

AUCHINLECK
ERASMUS
BELLAIRS

ANSTRUTHER
Bronkhorstspruit

F JOUBERT

Heidelberg

CRONJE
WINSLOE
Potchefstroom

Vaal

Standerton

Usutu

LOMBAARD
MONTAGUE
JOUBERT
(2000)
Laing's Nek
Majuba

SAUNDERS
VAN STADEN
Wakkerstroom

Phongola

Schuinshoogte (Ingogo)

17 Feb. 1881:
'Indian Column'
reinforcements
reach Newcastle

Newcastle

N.F.F.
COLLEY
(1462)

ORANGE
FREE STATE

ZULULAND

Drakensberg

Mzinyathi

Ladysmith

NATAL

Thukela

N

Caledon

BASUTOLAND

Pietermaritzburg

INDIAN
OCEAN

| 0 | 20 | 40 | 60 | 80 Miles |

| 0 | 50 | 100 Km |

Orange

Durban

25-30 Jan. 1881:
First reinforcements
arrive from India

Boer intentions as Lanyon. On 16 November he requested permission to move three companies from outlying garrisons into Pretoria, but Lanyon objected. However, a week later the movement of troops was approved, and Bellairs issued orders for one company of the 94th Regiment and a small mounted detachment from Marabastad, the mounted troop of the 94th Regiment at Wakkerstroom and the HQ and two companies of the 94th Regiment based at Lydenburg to move to Pretoria. Lanyon now began to recognise that tension was increasing and requested Colley to send the 58th Regiment to the Transvaal from Natal to help prevent any further civil disturbances. Colley refused at first but then relented. The 58th occupied Newcastle, Wakkerstroom and Standerton, allowing the garrisons of these towns to join the concentration of troops at Pretoria. But before these moves could be completed, the war had begun, forcing the companies of the 94th from Newcastle and Wakkerstroom to join their comrades at Standerton.

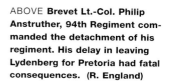

ABOVE **Brevet Lt.-Col. Philip Anstruther, 94th Regiment commanded the detachment of his regiment. His delay in leaving Lydenberg for Pretoria had fatal consequences. (R. England)**

BELOW **A Boer commandant. A typical Boer of the period, he is carrying the popular .500/.450 Westley Richards falling block breech-loading rifle.**

THE BOER PLAN

The mass meeting at Paardekraal marked the end of Boer attempts to negotiate a settlement with the British authorities. The feelings of the people were clear: about 4,000 attended the meeting and voted overwhelmingly for the restoration of the Republic. When the meeting was concluded, the women and children returned to their farms while the men formed into commandos. One group proceeded to Potchefstroom to arrange the printing of the declaration of independence, another went to Heidelberg to establish a new capital, since the British were occupying Pretoria. The newly elected Boer Triumvirate knew of the British decision to increase the troop strength in Pretoria, and to prevent this consolidation of the British garrison two commandos were despatched to intercept these movements.

By the end of December the Boers had besieging forces surrounding all the isolated British garrisons in the Transvaal. With these garrisons now unable to interfere with Boer plans, Commandant-General Piet Joubert rode south to the Transvaal-Natal border and tentatively crossed on 1 January 1881. A few miles south of the border lay Laing's Nek, an extended spur of the Drakensberg mountains. When the British moved up to relieve the garrisons in the Transvaal they would be forced to follow the road from Newcastle that crossed the Nek. This road provided the only practical route into the Transvaal for a heavily laden British column, so Laing's Nek provided a perfect position from which Joubert could oppose any such move.

OPENING MOVES

THE MARCH TO PRETORIA

he orders issued by Bellairs to authorise the movement of elements of the 94th Regiment from Marabastad, Wakkerstroom and Lydenburg were despatched from Pretoria on 23 November 1880. The instructions were received in Lydenburg, 188 miles away, by Lieutenant-Colonel Anstruther on 27 November. Anstruther had been in the isolated garrison at Lydenburg for almost a year, and was delighted at the prospect of moving to Pretoria. The wagons required for this movement had to be hired from local civilians, who were rather reluctant to pass their property to the safe-keeping of the military, and

Bronkhorstspruit, showing the road along which Anstruther's column was marching. Still lying on the road are the bones of some of the cattle shot in the attack and two flattened foreign service helmets. (Natal Archives, Pietermaritzburg)

The mass grave of NCOs and men killed at Bronkhorstspruit. The ridge in the distance is where the Boers first appeared before advancing to the thin screen of trees from where they opened fire. (Natal Archives, Pietermaritzburg)

Anstruther's departure until 5 December. However, part of this delay was caused by Anstruther's demand for wagons beyond the number to which his command was entitled. Regulations allowed the column 10 or 11 ox wagons, but Anstruther acquired 29 transport wagons in addition to two mule carts, an ox-drawn ambulance, a water cart and a further ox wagon to carry the regimental canteen – a total of 34 vehicles. A garrison of about 50 men remained. The column was strung out for well over a mile on the road; accompanying the wagons were 268 men of all ranks, three women and two children.

The day after Anstruther started his march rain set in, turning the dirt roads into liquid mud and making progress slow. In Pretoria the authorities were growing concerned. On 10 December the company from Marabastad completed their 155-mile march, but four days later Anstruther had only reached Middelburg and was still 97 miles short of Pretoria. On 17 December Anstruther received a communication from Pretoria. Although there had been no declaration of hostilities, the letter warned him that a large body of Boers had left their camp for an unknown destination. It went on to advise him to guard against a surprise attack on the march. Anstruther acknowledged receipt of the letter and continued his slow progress.

Strength of British Column at Bronkhorstspruit 20 December 1880

	Officers	Men
94th Regiment	6	246
Army Service Corps	2	10
Army Hospital Corps	1	3
Total	9	259

The grave of officers killed at Bronkhorstspruit. Anstruther's grave is marked with the large headstone. He was shot five times and died six days later following the amputation of one of his legs. (Natal Archives, Pietermaritzburg)

The march on 20 December started like any other. Anstruther had only four mounted infantry to act as scouts, two operating to the front of the column and two towards the rear. Between 300 and 400 yards behind the leading scouts rode Lieutenant-Colonel Anstruther, Captain J.M. Elliot, Lieutenant and Adjutant H.A.C. Harrison and Conductor R. Egerton of the Army Service Corps. Behind these officers marched the band, about 40 strong, playing various popular tunes, followed by F Company, 94th Regiment, also with about 40 men. Next came a colour party of five and A Company, 94th Regiment with 38 men. Between these men and the long straggling convoy of 34 wagons marched 21 men of the Quarter Guard and a Provost Escort of five men with 18 prisoners. Some 200–300 yards behind the last of the wagons was a rearguard of 20 men. The

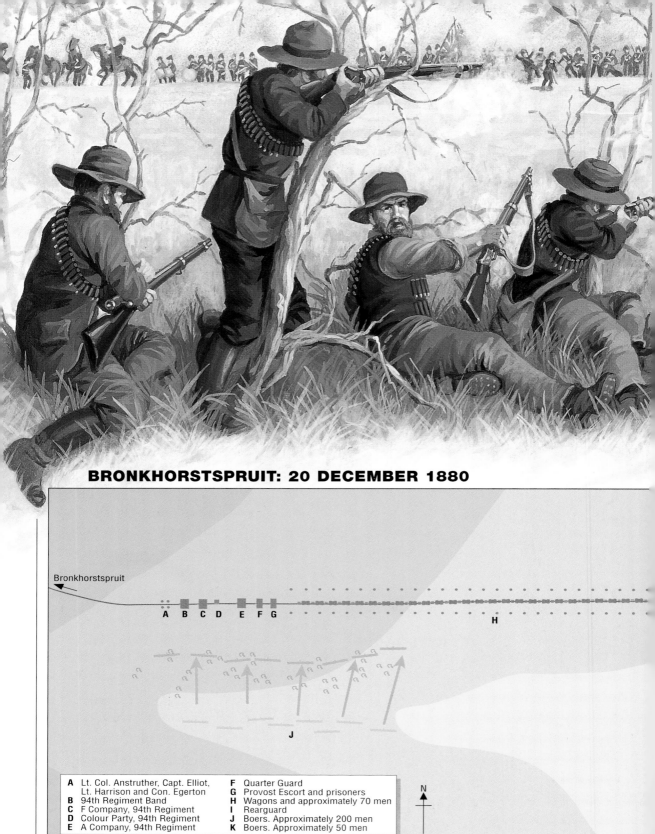

BRONKHORSTSPRUIT: 20 DECEMBER 1880

Bronkhorstspruit

A B C D E F G

H

J

N

A	Lt. Col. Anstruther, Capt. Elliot, Lt. Harrison and Con. Egerton	**F**	Quarter Guard
B	94th Regiment Band	**G**	Provost Escort and prisoners
C	F Company, 94th Regiment	**H**	Wagons and approximately 70 men
D	Colour Party, 94th Regiment	**I**	Rearguard
E	A Company, 94th Regiment	**J**	Boers. Approximately 200 men
		K	Boers. Approximately 50 men

BOERS AT BRONKHORSTSPRUIT

On 20 December 1880 a column of the 94th Regiment marching to Pretoria was attacked at Bronkhorstspruit. Making use of the limited cover the Boers crept forward, opening fire at about 200 yards. The British, surprised by this aggressive move, suffered terrible casualties, forcing their wounded commanding officer to surrender.

Middelburg

I

K

Ox wagons
Individual soldiers
Scattered thorn bush

ll units drawn to approximately
epresent actual strength

250		500 yds
250		500 m

remainder of Anstruther's force were thinly spread on either side of the wagons, but there were no outlying flank guards.

At about 12.30pm the column was about two miles from Bronkhorstspruit, where they intended to make camp that night. The country at this point is mainly flat. To the right of the road several farms dotted the landscape, each masked by a line of trees. To the left of the road, at a distance of about 500 yards, ran a low grassy ridge. Extending from the base of the ridge to within about 200 yards of the road was a thin screen of thorn trees. Concealed behind this ridge was a commando led by Commandant Frans Joubert with orders to prevent Anstruther from reaching Pretoria.

THE ACTION AT BRONKHORSTSPRUIT

The column moved slowly on until suddenly the band stopped playing and all eyes turned to the left. As if from nowhere a group of about 150 mounted Boers had appeared, lining the crest of the low ridge. **25**

Anstruther turned his horse back to the column, dismounted and ordered the men and wagons to close up. At the same time a lone rider emerged from the thorn trees and rode forward under a white flag. He stopped some distance off and was met by Conductor Egerton, the senior warrant officer, to whom he handed a letter. Anstruther then walked up and took the letter. It informed him that the Transvaal had been declared a Republic and that until a reply had been received from Lanyon it was not known whether a state of war existed. In the circumstances Anstruther was required to hold his position; if he chose to continue his march to Pretoria, it would be considered a declaration of war. The messenger added that two minutes only were to be allowed for his reply. Anstruther informed the messenger that his orders were to go to Pretoria and that that was what he intended doing. He then asked the messenger if he would pass this reply to his commander to which the messenger agreed.

While this parley had been in progress, the number of Boers on the ridge had increased greatly, and many began to filter forward through the thorn trees to a position about 200 yards from the column. A certain nervousness now set in on both sides. Anstruther and Egerton turned to walk back to the road as the Boer messenger galloped off towards the ridge, but observing the Boers closing in on the column Anstruther began to run. As he reached the column, the wagons had still not closed up; he shouted orders to F Company to form into skirmish order but before they could complete their deployment a murderous volley crashed out from the Boer riflemen concealed in the trees. The exposed infantry dived for the ground but were hopelessly exposed. Within the first few minutes all but one of the nine officers was dead or wounded.

The colours of the 94th were saved by Conductor Egerton, who hid them under his coat. This photo shows them displayed with the colours of the 2/21st in Pretoria. The Queen's Colour of the 94th, the lower of the two right-hand colours, appears badly damaged. (Africana Museum, Johannesburg)

Following news of the Boer attack at Bronkhorstspruit, large numbers of reinforcements were ordered to Natal from Britain and India. Once safely ashore, the arduous journey upcountry began.

Anstruther himself was shot five times in the legs. Then the oxen were picked off and anyone who moved near the ammunition wagons was shot down. The carnage was astounding: within about 15 minutes 156 men and one woman were either dead or wounded, a casualty rate of 58 per cent.

Although Anstruther was severely wounded he was aware of the impossible situation his men were in and so gave the order for them to surrender. The scene on the road was horrendous: lifeless soldiers in all the postures of death and boys from the band lying motionless in congealing pools of blood. The pleas of the wounded, mingled with the pitiful moans of the dying oxen and horses, filled the air. Surgeon Ward, the senior medical officer with the column, reported that the average number of wounds per man was five. Conductor Egerton, who was himself wounded, got permission to walk the 38 miles to Pretoria to arrange medical help. With Sergeant Bradley he arrived safely in the early hours of the next morning, having managed to save the 94th's colours by wrapping them around his body under his jacket. On 26 December Lieutenant-Colonel Anstruther died following the amputation of one of his legs. The number of Boers who took part in the attack is impossible to determine. Boer sources state that their numbers were roughly equal to the British, but British sources give the number as between 1,000 and 1,200 – although this may be partly due to the British belief that their high casualties must have been caused by a superiority of numbers. There is similar confusion over Boer casualties. Boer figures state there were only two dead and five wounded, while one British sergeant claims he saw 44 bodies awaiting burial at two nearby farms.

The Natal Field Force

The news of the Bronkhorstspruit disaster appalled and shocked the British. Lanyon immediately declared martial law and prepared Pretoria for a siege, sending word by a circuitous route to Colley, who received it on 25 December. When news reached London, orders were issued for a number of reinforcements to be despatched to Africa from home and from India. While Colley was now rapidly organising his limited military strength, two ships docked at Durban carrying large drafts for the regiments already stationed there. In this way 148 men arrived for the 58th, 94th and 91st (stationed at Cape Town) and 209 men for the 3/60th and 2/21st. A few days later, on 5 January, HMS *Boadicea* arrived at Durban, and the following day it responded to Colley's request for assistance by assembling a Naval Brigade of five officers and 124 petty officers and men, with two Gatling guns and three 24-pdr rocket tubes. These men were placed under orders, and all except the 91st were despatched to the northern Natal town of Newcastle, where the Natal Field Force was being assembled to relieve the Transvaal garrisons which by now were all under siege. The reinforcements marched into the camp at Fort Amiel in Newcastle on 19 January, and five days later the whole force was ready to march towards the Transvaal, led by Colley but under the nominal command of Colonel B.M. Deane.

Natal Field Force
24 January 1881

	Officers	Other Ranks	Total
Staff	3	1	4
Mounted Squadron	6	124	130
Natal Mounted Police	3	58	61
Royal Artillery	4	75	79
Royal Engineers	1	6	7
2/21st Regt.	2	80	82
58th Regt. (HQ & 5 coys.)	15	487	502
3/60th Rifles (HQ & 5 coys.)	17	411	428
Army Service Corps	3	11	14
Ordnance	1	0	1
Army Medical Dept.	5	0	5
Army Hospital Corps	0	22	22
Naval Brigade	5	122	127
Total	65	1,397	1,462

Royal Artillery
N/5 Two 9-pdr RML.
10/7 Two 9-pdr RML.
3/60th Two 7-pdr RML.

Naval Brigade
Gatling guns (2)
24-pdr rocket tubes (3)

THE BATTLE OF LAING'S NEK

THE BRITISH ADVANCE TO MOUNT PROSPECT

Colley was somewhat confused by this sudden turn of events and was unsure of his next step. He regarded the defeat of the 94th at Bronkhorstspruit 'like Isandlwana on a smaller scale' and felt that steps had to be taken quickly to repair the damage done to British prestige. Although he knew large numbers of reinforcements were on their way to him, he realised that time was against him; no one knew just how long the isolated Transvaal garrisons could hold out. The Boers held all of the Transvaal except for these points, and if any should fall it would be disastrous, possibly encouraging support from Boer sympathisers in the Cape Colony, Orange Free State, Natal and even overseas. Colley therefore decided upon a quick, bold movement into the Transvaal with the force available, prior to the arrival of reinforcements. This would ease the situation for his besieged garrisons as numbers of Boers would have to be called forward to oppose his advance. In London there were many high-ranking officials who doubted the wisdom of this plan, but Colley was convinced of his ability to inflict defeat upon the Boers, who had been pilloried in the British press with accusations of 'deliberate treachery' and 'cold-blooded murder' after Bronkhorstspruit.

The day before the Natal Field Force marched from Newcastle, Colley sent an ultimatum to the Boers ordering them, as insurgents, to disperse. The ultimatum reached Joubert, who sent it on to Heidelberg. The Boer reply, which varied little from previous communications, was not returned to Joubert until after events had taken a further dramatic turn.

A reconnaissance party of the Natal Mounted Police, led by Brevet Major Poole, RA, found Laing's Nek unoccupied on 19 January. This illustration is based on Poole's sketch. He was killed at Laing's Nek nine days later.

For three days before Colley set out it had rained heavily, and this made the column's progress both slow and exhausting. On the second day the most difficult part of the march was encountered, the long climb up to a rocky hill known as Schuinshoogte. Camp was made at the Ingogo river beyond. From here the column had a magnificent view of the Drakensberg mountains and the dramatic twin buttresses of Nkwelo and Majuba. Crossing the river the next morning was a prelude to another exhausting day for the men of the Natal Field Force. They covered another five miles of difficult country, to Mount Prospect, where mist and rain forced them to halt, form wagon laager and make camp for the night. The next morning, 27 January, heralded more heavy rain and a thick mist, and the column was forced to remain in position, though it did allow the men some much needed rest.

THE BOER ADVANCE TO LAING'S NEK

The Boers, under Piet Joubert, had arrived at the Transvaal-Natal border on 1 January and set up camp just inside Natal, at a tiny settlement named Coldstream. From here daily patrols extended through the surrounding countryside and to Laing's Nek, a short distance to the south. Laing's Nek was the perfect defensive position in the district. The border of Natal narrows to a point in this area, flanked to the west by the Orange Free State and to the north and east by the Transvaal. The road leading into the Transvaal is overlooked to the west by the imposing peak of Majuba from which extends a long spur running west to east over which the road passes. The end of this ridge curves to the south, and any movement further east is curtailed by the valley of the Buffalo (Mzinyathi) river. As soon as Commandant-General Joubert heard of Colley's forward movement from Newcastle he began to advance some of his commandos to Laing's Nek, where they formed two new laagers on either side of the road on the reverse slopes. On the day that Colley made camp at Mount Prospect, about 1,000 Boers were at the Nek; this number had doubled by 28 January. Joubert had immediately given orders for trenches to be dug, and stones piled to build sangers and walls along the Boer position. The killing ground was obvious: any force attacking the Nek would be completely exposed to fire from at least two sides.

COLLEY'S PLAN OF ATTACK

At 6.15am on the morning of Friday 28 January Colley's force, detailed for the attack on Laing's Nek, marched out of the camp at Mount Prospect. The previous evening Colley had informed his senior officers of his plan. Having observed the Laing's Nek position closely, Colley announced that it was his intention to first attract the Boers' attention by opening fire on the long ridge (which the British called Table Mountain) with his artillery and rockets from a low spur of Majuba. The artillery were to be supported by the Natal Mounted Police, the Naval Brigade and the 3/60th. From there this part of the force would be in a position to threaten the Nek. Once this position was secure, the 58th Regiment were to advance up a steep spur of Table Mountain, at the eastern end, re-form and then turn to their left and sweep along the heights towards the road at the Nek. If the advance was threatened on its right flank as it climbed the spur, a company was to be despatched in that direction where the Mounted Squadron, ascending the hills further to the right, would be able to attack the enemy's left flank. With the enemy then in retreat, the artillery would be able to move up onto the Nek and, in conjunction with the Mounted Squadron, harry the Boers as they retreated.

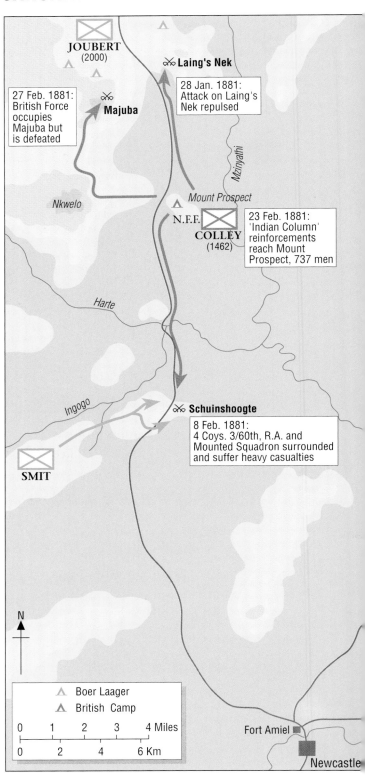

THE MAJUBA CAMPAIGN JANUARY-FEBRUARY 1881

JOUBERT (2000)

Laing's Nek

27 Feb. 1881: British Force occupies Majuba but is defeated

Majuba

28 Jan. 1881: Attack on Laing's Nek repulsed

Mzinyathi

Nkwelo

Mount Prospect

N.F.F.

COLLEY (1462)

23 Feb. 1881: 'Indian Column' reinforcements reach Mount Prospect, 737 men

Harte

Schuinshoogte

8 Feb. 1881: 4 Coys. 3/60th, R.A. and Mounted Squadron surrounded and suffer heavy casualties

Ingogo

SMIT

N

Boer Laager
British Camp

0 1 2 3 4 Miles
0 2 4 6 Km

Fort Amiel

Newcastle

On 27 January Colley spent much of the day observing the Boer positions on Laing's Nek through his binoculars. The Boers were still busily entrenching. Colley decided upon an attack against the Boer extreme left. (R. England)

Laing's Nek today, looking along the heights towards the east. The slopes were open grassland at the time. The bare slope, left centre, is the one up which the 58th attacked. The rounded hill on the right is that attacked by the Mounted Squadron.

British Force at Battle of Laing's Nek, 28 January 1881

	Officers	Other Ranks	Total
Staff	9	0	9
Mounted Squadron	6	113	119
Natal Mounted Police	3	63	66
Royal Artillery	4	72	76
Royal Engineers	1	0	1
2/21st Regt.	1	6	7
58th Regt. (HQ & 5 coys.)	14	479	493
3/60th Rifles (HQ & 4 coys.)	12	321	333
Army Medical Dept.	4	0	4
Army Hospital Corps	0	20	20
Naval Brigade	4	84	88
Total	58	1158	1216

The force was accompanied by four 9-pdrs, two 7-pdrs and three 24-pdr rocket tubes.

Boer Force at Battle of Laing's Nek, 28 January 1881

It is impossible to be precise when discussing Boer numbers at Laing's Nek, or to determine which commandos were present. It is estimated that Commandant-General Joubert had about 2,000 Boers in the area of the action, but these were distributed along the whole Boer defensive position, enabling only part of the force to engage the British – perhaps as little as 400.

At 9.20am all Colley's men were in position. About 1,500 yards from the Nek a company of 3/60th formed in extended order. To their left, also in extended order, stood the Naval Brigade with their rocket tubes on the extreme left, sheltered by a stone wall near Laing's farm. About 200 yards further back were the other three companies of 3/60th, standing just below the crest of the low spur running from Majuba. On the summit of the spur were the six artillery pieces. A little further back the 58th awaited the order to advance, with the Mounted Squadron to their right rear and the Natal Mounted Police on the left rear.

THE BATTLE OPENS

At about 9.25am the order was given for the artillery and rockets to open fire on the Boer positions on the Nek and reverse slope. All eyes followed the erratic path of the rockets as the air filled with their high-pitched shrieks and the dull thud of the artillery. The Boers took cover in their trenches and behind their breastworks. The British firmly believed that the Boers greatly feared the use of artillery, but there was no great panic. A few Boers were observed galloping madly about but the majority sat out the bombardment. While this was going on, Colley ordered forward his infantry on the right to begin the turning movement that would roll up the Boer position.

Brownlow's Charge

At about 9.40am Major William Hingeston led the 58th Regiment forward. Rather unusually, Colley then directed five of his staff, including Colonel Deane who nominally commanded the Natal Field Force, to accompany the 58th. Deane immediately took command of the attack. From their start position it was about 1,000 yards to the beginning of the spur which led up to Table Mountain and the Boer positions. The advance

Plate

I.

ABOVE **Having struggled up the spur leading to Table Mountain, the 58th found themselves still more than 150 yards from the Boer positions. Colonel Deane of the staff, on horseback, led the regiment forward across the glacis-like slope. The attack failed and Deane was killed. (I. Knight)**

LEFT **Lance-Corporal William Clarke, KDG was shot in the left elbow during Brownlow's charge. The bullet smashed bones in the upper arm but after an operation he was able to continue an active life, although one arm was shorter than the other. (Royal College of Surgeons)**

was not straightforward as two other spurs and two streams had to be crossed before they reached it. The 58th were supported on their right flank by the Mounted Squadron, commanded by Major William Brownlow of the 1st King's Dragoon Guards (KDG). This scratch force, formed for the campaign, had only had limited time for training. At 10.10am, as the 58th begin their advance up the spur in a tightly packed column of companies, four abreast, they came under fire from a few Boer skirmishers. The Boers were on the slopes of a round-topped hill which marked the extreme southeastern point of the Boer position. The range was about 900 yards and the firing largely ineffective. Brownlow's orders were to protect the flank of the 58th if they came under attack, and rather than waiting to check for the most suitable approach to the Boer position, he immediately wheeled his men to the right and prepared to attack up the hill. Unfortunately Brownlow's impetuosity forced him to lead his men up the steepest part of the hill, and most of the horses were blown before they had clambered half-way to the top. Brownlow, with Troop Sergeant-Major Lunny, KDG, were the first to reach the crest of the ridge held by the Boers, followed by the rest of the first troop. The second troop were still struggling up behind. A volley crashed out from the Boer defenders, and Brownlow's horse collapsed to the ground. Lunny reached the Boer position, firing his revolver in all directions. He killed one Boer and wounded another before he was shot dead. The scene on the ridge was one of total confusion. Wounded horses, terrified and exhausted, wheeled about uncontrollably while unseated riders desperately attempted to make good their escape. Amid this confusion an act of coolness and bravery shone out. Brownlow's servant, Private John Doogan, KDG, had been wounded in the charge, but seeing his master unhorsed close to the enemy, he dismounted and pressed Brownlow to take his own steed, during which time Doogan was again wounded. Incredibly both men escaped. It appears that an attempt was made to

BATTLE OF LAING'S NEK

The morning of 28th January 1881, 09.25-12.00 viewed from the south-west showing the British attack and Boer counterattack

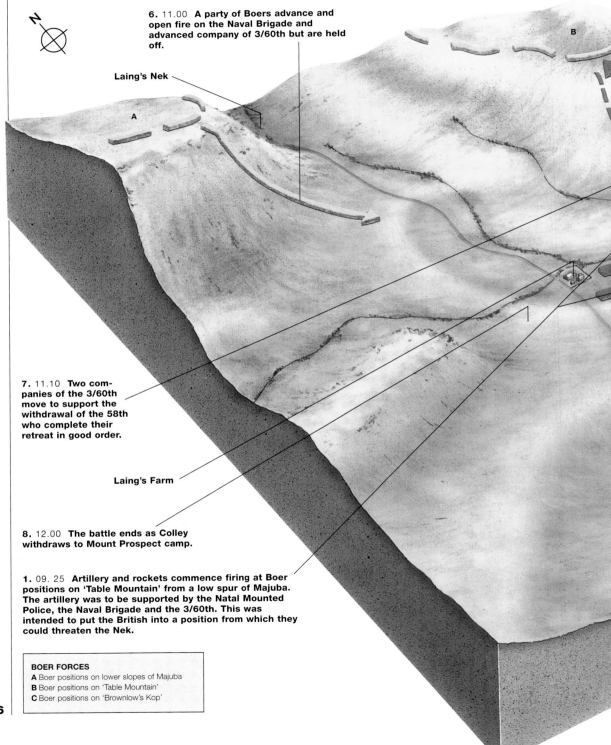

X
JOUBERT

6. 11.00 **A party of Boers advance and open fire on the Naval Brigade and advanced company of 3/60th but are held off.**

Laing's Nek

A

B

7. 11.10 **Two companies of the 3/60th move to support the withdrawal of the 58th who complete their retreat in good order.**

Laing's Farm

8. 12.00 **The battle ends as Colley withdraws to Mount Prospect camp.**

1. 09. 25 **Artillery and rockets commence firing at Boer positions on 'Table Mountain' from a low spur of Majuba. The artillery was to be supported by the Natal Mounted Police, the Naval Brigade and the 3/60th. This was intended to put the British into a position from which they could threaten the Nek.**

BOER FORCES
A Boer positions on lower slopes of Majuba
B Boer positions on 'Table Mountain'
C Boer positions on 'Brownlow's Kop'

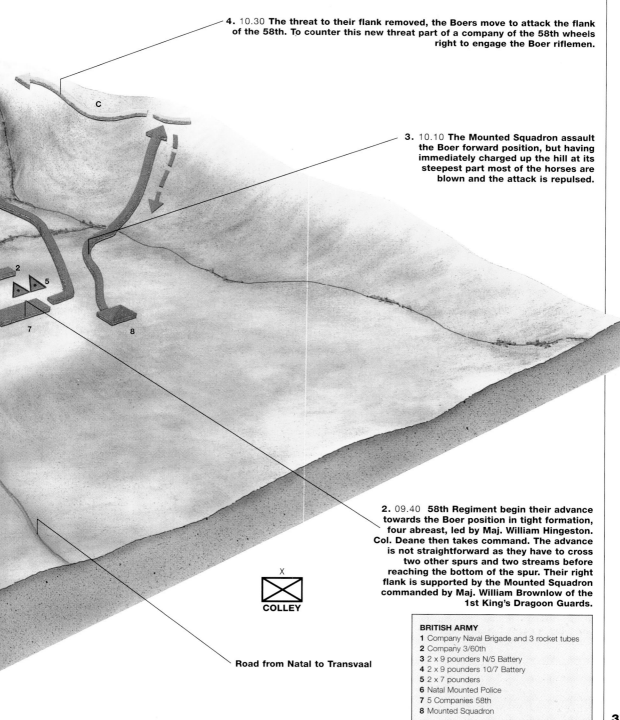

5. 11.00 Reaching the top of the slope the 58th are confronted with an entrenched Boer position about 160 yards away. During their charge on the Boer entrenchment both Col. Deane and Maj. Hingeston are killed. The 58th are forced to retire pursued by the Boers. One company of the 58th put up an effective rearguard action.

4. 10.30 The threat to their flank removed, the Boers move to attack the flank of the 58th. To counter this new threat part of a company of the 58th wheels right to engage the Boer riflemen.

3. 10.10 The Mounted Squadron assault the Boer forward position, but having immediately charged up the hill at its steepest part most of the horses are blown and the attack is repulsed.

C

2

5

7

8

2. 09.40 58th Regiment begin their advance towards the Boer position in tight formation, four abreast, led by Maj. William Hingeston. Col. Deane then takes command. The advance is not straightforward as they have to cross two other spurs and two streams before reaching the bottom of the spur. Their right flank is supported by the Mounted Squadron commanded by Maj. William Brownlow of the 1st King's Dragoon Guards.

X

COLLEY

Road from Natal to Transvaal

BRITISH ARMY
1 Company Naval Brigade and 3 rocket tubes
2 Company 3/60th
3 2 x 9 pounders N/5 Battery
4 2 x 9 pounders 10/7 Battery
5 2 x 7 pounders
6 Natal Mounted Police
7 5 Companies 58th
8 Mounted Squadron

LEFT **As the 58th charged into the Boer fire, Lieutenant Monck's horse was shot from under him. Lieutenant Elwes, a fellow old Etonian and Colley's ADC, then rode past and shouted: 'Come along Monck! Floreat Etona! We must be in the front rank.' Seconds later Elwes was dead; Monck survived. (I. Knight)**

rally the shattered first troop, but this failed to achieve any worthwhile results since half of the horses were dead or wounded. Meanwhile the second troop, disconcerted by the firing and fleeing horses ahead of them, turned before reaching the crest and retreated down the hill. Brownlow was apparently disgusted with the performance of these men and felt so let down that he refused to speak to them when they returned to camp. However, had Brownlow not rushed into the attack but proceeded a little further with the 58th, he would have found a much gentler slope by which he could have assaulted the Boer position. After the battle, the hill was named 'Brownlow's Kop' by the British.

The Repulse of the 58th Regiment

The impact of Brownlow's failure to clear the Boer position now began to take effect. Those Boers freed by the retreat of the mounted men were able to move to a new position and open fire on the 58th Regiment below.

All through the mounted charge the infantry had struggled up the increasingly difficult slopes of the spur. Its steepness had been deceptive through Colley's field glasses, and although the long slippery grass which

RIGHT **Contemporary images of heroism. Colonel Deane, unhorsed, continues to lead the advance of the 58th before his death. Private Doogan, KDG, although wounded himself, insists that Major Brownlow takes his horse. Lieutenant Hill, 58th, winning the Victoria Cross for rescuing wounded comrades during the retreat. (R. England)**

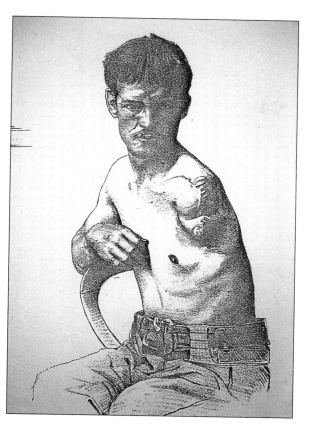

cloaked the slope had provided handholds as the breathless infantry clambered up the one in 15 gradient, it had also clung to their ankles and brought them crashing to the ground. The horsemanship of the officers was severely tested as they moved upwards in leaps and bounds.

To counter the new threat to their flank, part of a company of the 58th wheeled to the right to engage the Boer riflemen while Colonel Deane urged the rest of the column on up the slope. Leading from the front, at about 10.40am Deane reached the ridge where the spur joined Table Mountain. Too late he realised his error in not extending the companies to right and left. As his panting and exhausted compressed column reached the crest, they found themselves confronted with a glacis-like slope which led up to an entrenched Boer position about 160 yards away. Deane immediately shouted out for the men to extend to the right and left and fix bayonets. The British exchanged shots with the Boers for about five minutes, but in their congested position were obviously getting the worst of the action. To rectify this situation Colonel Deane, still mounted, gave the order for the 58th to charge the Boer entrenchment. Deane, who was seeing action for

COL. DEANE.   PRIVATE DOOGEN'S HEROISM.   LIEUT. HILL.

BROWNLOW'S CHARGE AT LAING'S NEK
The Mounted Squadron carried out an uphill charge against a group of Boers at
Laing's Nek. On reaching the summit they found the Boers lining a prepared
position on the reverse slope. The first troop was thrown into disarry by
enemy fire while the second troop refused to follow up.

the first time, presented an easy target as the bullets flew all around, within seconds he was down. Undeterred he leapt to his feet, shouted: 'I am all right!' and led the 58th forward. Again he was cut down, and this time he did not rise. Lieutenant Inman of the 3/60th, Deane's orderly officer, was shot just behind him. Major Hingeston, now commanding his regiment again, urged the men on into the withering fire and fell mortally wounded about the same time that Major Poole and Lieutenant Elwes, both of Colley's staff, were shot dead. Of the five members of

Dead and wounded men of the 58th Regiment at the battle of Laing's Nek. The Boers stripped the dead of their boots, leggings and accoutrements, but generally treated the wounded well.
(R. England)

Colley's staff that had joined the attack on Laing's Nek, four were now dead. The only survivor was Major Essex, who amazingly had been one of the five imperial officers to survive the crushing defeat at Isandlwana in the Zulu War two years earlier. Incredibly the 58th had reached as close as 30 or 40 yards to the Boer position in places but could advance no further. Keeping close to the ground they continued to fire at the Boers. Major Hingeston was succeeded in command of the 58th by Captain Lovegrove, but he too soon fell wounded. Temporarily the command of the 58th fell to Lieutenant S. Jopp.

Boer reinforcements had been fed into the front line all through the action, and it was now obvious that the attack could not succeed. Just after 11.00am Major Essex gave the order for the retreat to commence, and slowly the 58th fell back to the ridge of the mountain, the three right-hand companies first followed by the two left-hand companies. As they crossed the ridge the artillery below recommenced their bombardment (which had halted as the 58th had begun to climb up the spur). The fire was accurate, but a number of British wounded on the hill were probably killed by it. After a short rest out of the fire to their front, the 58th began to retire down the spur in good order.

Saving the Colours

The Boers now moved from their cover for the first time and pursued the retreating 58th. In addition, a party moved against the 3/60th and Naval Brigade on the British left flank, but they were held off. As the 58th moved down the slope, they were still under fire from all sides. Lieutenant Baillie, who had been carrying the Regimental Colour during the battle, was wounded. Lieutenant Peel, who carried the Queen's Colour, offered to assist his comrade, but Baillie refused, only asking that the Colours should be saved. Peel took them both up but shortly after tripped and fell; the Colours were taken on by a sergeant and Peel recovered them later. While this was going on, Lieutenant Hill attempted to rescue the wounded Lieutenant Baillie. Unable to lift him into the saddle, Hill carried his fellow officer down the spur, but while struggling down Baillie received another wound which proved fatal. Undeterred, Hill returned up the hill twice more and rescued two wounded men, for which gallant conduct he was awarded the Victoria Cross.

The retreat down the spur was a very orderly affair considering what the regiment had just been through. One company had formed, turned to face the Boers and put up a very effective rearguard action. At the commencement of the retreat two companies of the 3/60th were moved across to cover the movement and attempt to pin down the Boer pursuers. On reaching the foot of the spur safely, the regiment re-formed and marched back to its start position 'with as erect and soldierly bearing, as when it marched out'. With the main attack having failed, the

forward troops on the left were withdrawn and the whole force retired to Mount Prospect camp in two sections.

Besides having his staff virtually wiped out, Colley lost a total of seven officers and 77 men killed, three officers and 110 men wounded and two prisoners. The 58th lost the majority of these casualties, 74 killed and 101 wounded, 35 per cent of their total strength. The Boers gave their casualties as 14 killed and 27 wounded.

Safely back in camp, that evening Colley called his command together and made a short address. In it he personally accepted the blame for the repulse, totally exonerating the 58th. He then added: 'We certainly shall take possession of that hill eventually, and I sincerely hope that all those men who have so nobly done their duty today will be with me then.' But Colley's last comment, which may reveal the key to his future planning, was perhaps a contributing factor to a far greater tragedy that had yet to unfold.

There was little now that Colley could do. With Colonel Deane's death, he now officially assumed command of the Natal Field Force and moved the camp about 500 yards, to a better position, and strengthened his outlying defences. He hoped that the Boers would attack his well defended camp, but he knew there was very little chance that they would be so rash. The Natal Mounted Police were sent back to Newcastle to bolster the garrison and ensure that communications could be kept open between there and Mount Prospect. All that was then left to do was to await the arrival of reinforcements. Then he could return to the offensive, clear Laing's Nek and relieve the besieged garrisons in the Transvaal.

Reinforcements Despatched

When word of the attack on the 94th Regiment at Bronkhorstspruit was received in London, no effort was spared in getting reinforcements to Natal as fast as possible. On 6 January General Sir Evelyn Wood was appointed as Colley's second-in-command. Wood, a veteran of many

One of the seven mass graves of the 58th located by the author in 1994. This grave lies high up the spur. The background is dominated by the looming presence of Majuba.

A contemporary photograph of the monument to the fallen of the 58th Regiment. Erected at the top of the spur, it is now surrounded by forestry trees. (Natal Museum, Pietermaritzburg)

trying campaigns, was actually senior in army rank to Colley, but agreed to accept the position. The choice was a good one, since Wood had enhanced his own reputation two years earlier in the war against the Zulus and had gained the respect of the British soldiers and Boers alike. Wood embarked from England on 14 January. On 25 January the first of Colley's reinforcements arrived from India. First to land were the 2/60th Rifles, the 15th Hussars and an artillery battery. Five days later they were joined by the 83rd and 92nd regiments and a second Naval Brigade of 58 men, drawn from HMS *Dido* and HMS *Boadicea*, with two 9-pdr guns. As soon as word reached the reinforcements of Colley's repulse at Laing's Nek, they were ordered up to Newcastle, dropping off the 83rd on the way a few miles south of Pietermaritzburg.

THE ATTACK OF THE
58TH AT LAING'S NEK
Having failed to clear the Boer
positions at Laing's Nek the 58th
Regiment were forced to retire.
During the retreat the Colours
provided a tempting target for Boer
marksmen. Despite his wounds Lieutenant
Baillie succeeded in handing the Regimental
Colour to Lieutenant Peel, who carried both
colours to safety.

LEFT General Sir Evelyn Wood VC KCB. On 6 January
Wood was appointed Colley's second in command,
although senior in army rank. He did not reach Natal until
February; by then Colley had fought a second engagement.

BATTLE OF
SCHUINSHOOGTE (Ingogo)

THREAT TO COMMUNICATIONS

The road between Mount Prospect and Newcastle was just under 20 miles long. It passed up and down tortuous hills and through difficult river crossings but it was an essential link for Colley's force. Along this single muddy track passed all his correspondence, food, medical requirements and ammunition. (So far telegraphic communications with Newcastle had not been interfered with by the Boers.) It therefore became increasingly more annoying for Colley to have roving bands of the enemy interfering with this important but exposed route. On 7 February the Boers became bolder. About mid-morning one of the camp's regular post deliveries to Newcastle departed. As usual the letters were escorted by a detachment of six men from the Mounted Squadron, but on the way they were intercepted by a party of about 50 Boers who opened fire. The post detail turned and rode back across the Ingogo river as fast as they could, all returning safely to Mount Prospect except one escort who managed to get through to Newcastle. The next morning Colley received a telegraph from Newcastle informing him that owing to increased Boer activity in the area it would be unwise to send forward the

Schuinshoogte was the highest point on the road between Newcastle and Mount Prospect. On first sighting the Boers, Colley distributed his men around the boulder-strewn plateau. This photo shows the boulders marking the perimeter. The Boers were positioned away to the right.

wagon convoy that Colley had been expecting to depart that day. Colley decided to remove this threat to his communications at once by making a demonstration in force along the Newcastle road, meeting his expected convoy in the process and bringing it in to camp.

Colley Moves to Clear the Road

Colley issued orders to prepare to march. The force was to consist of five companies of the 3/60th, part of the Mounted Squadron and four artillery pieces; the artillery alone, Colley felt, would discourage the Boers from interfering with his mission. So convinced was he that he would not encounter any problems on the march, that he gave no orders for rations to be issued and did not request a watercart to accompany the march. As they left camp, at 8.30am, Colley ordered dinner to be prepared for their return at 3.30pm. It was a pleasant sunny morning and everyone was 'in good spirits at the prospect of an outing'.

The first two or three miles of the track from the camp were fairly easy going, and then they reached the first of a series of ridges – spurs extending from Nkwelo mountain – which mark the beginning of the descent to the Ingogo river. There the road winds for another two miles down a long stony hill to the river. The river crossing itself has a double drift, with fords about 100 yards apart. Once across the river, the track takes a gentle rise and then climbs gradually for about a mile and a half, to the plateau above, known as Schuinshoogte.

British Force engaged at Schuinshoogte, 8 February 1881

	Officers	Other Ranks	Total
Staff	6	1	7
Mounted Squadron	4	40	* 44
N/5 RA. (2 x 9-pdrs)	2	28	30
3/60th Rifles (4 coys.)	11	295	306
2/21st Regt.	0	4	**4
Army Medical Dept.	1	0	1
Army Hospital Corps	0	1	1
Total	24	369	393

* The Mounted Squadron appear to have taken only 38 horses.
** These men acted as stretcher bearers.
These figures are extracted from *The Journal of the Natal Field Force*, compiled by Major Edward Essex, Colley's staff officer and deputy assistant adjutant-general.

Boer Forces engaged at Schuinshoogte, 8 February 1881

Again it is difficult to be precise with Boer numbers. Initially there were about 100 Boers in the immediate area, but numbers soon increased as the action became general. Commanded by Nicholas Smit, the force was reinforced throughout the day and by nightfall it is estimated that about 500 Boers were present.

Before commencing his march down the hill to the river, Colley halted and prudently detached the two 7-pdr guns and one company of the 3/60th. He then ordered up a company of the 58th to relieve these

men so they could rejoin the main force. From here the artillery could command the approaches to the river, should any Boers be moving in that direction from behind Nkwelo. Sending the Mounted Squadron ahead the rest of the column snaked down to the river where the water in both drifts was only about knee-high. Once safely across, the main body began to reorganise itself while the mounted men rode on up towards the plateau.

THE BOER ATTACK

The peace of the leisurely patrol was suddenly broken by the sound of gunfire from the direction of the scouts. Falling back, they informed Colley that there was a large body of Boers ahead. Wasting no time, Colley ordered his command up onto the heights, the Rifles leading, followed by the artillery and staff. The highest point was a plateau

roughly triangle-shaped, very flat, with a covering of short grass and a perimeter studded with rough outcrops of rock. The ground below the plateau was also littered with rock and had the added advantage of expanses of long grass, in some places four feet high. As the artillery came up onto the plateau a body of 100 Boers was observed on a low ridge about 1,000 yards to the right. The Boers made no move to retire, but watched Colley's force form up on the high ground. Seconds later a shell from the artillery arched in their direction. It caused the Boers to scatter for cover but passed high over its mark. A second shell was closer but also failed to hit the target. The Rifles now extended around the perimeter, on both sides of the guns, and added their firepower to the growing din. But Colley was now in for a surprise. Instead of the Boers dispersing, led by Nicholas Smit, they began to use the numerous folds in the ground to advance towards his position. Within a very short space of time more Boers appeared from cover and began to extend around the ridge, opening a fierce and accurate fire on the surprised British. To prevent themselves from being outflanked, those on the plateau extended further until the only open point was on the north-east section of the rough circle. The guns were repositioned so that one pointed southwards while the other was placed on the northernmost edge of the plateau. By 12.15pm firing was heavy all around the position. The Rifles were lying prone, taking advantage of what cover they could while bullets raked across the plateau splashing off the rocks or finding an exposed arm or leg of a British soldier. Horses that moved too close to the edge of the plateau were an easy target. The British attempted to pick off the Boer marksmen, but it became suicide to raise a head above the rocks. The artillerymen who fearlessly continued to serve their pieces became the focus of Boer fire. Captain Greer, serving the southern gun, was killed quite early in the battle while Lieutenant Parsons' gun, on the northern side, also attracted much Boer fire. In an attempt to ease this situation, Colley ordered Major Brownlow to charge the Boer riflemen to the north with the depleted Mounted Squadron. Brownlow's men moved forward to the edge of the plateau, but before they could charge, a volley crashed out from about 150 yards and decimated the mounted force. It appears that the Boers deliberately aimed at the horses, since half of them were hit while only one man was wounded. Brownlow, who had also survived the charge at Laing's Nek, brought his men back to the plateau and dismounted. The casualties continued to mount in the artillery, and it was not long before volunteers were called from the Rifles to take their place. Eventually Colley ordered the guns to withdraw a short distance, but this limited their field of fire, which became concentrated on Boer reinforcements moving towards the battlefield.

A Boer attempt to outflank the open British left flank at about 2.30pm was defeated, but with appalling casualties. Colley ordered a half company of the 3/60th to move out wide on the left to oppose this Boer movement. Led into

49

BATTLE OF SCHUINSHOOGTE (INGOGO): 8 FEBRUARY 1881

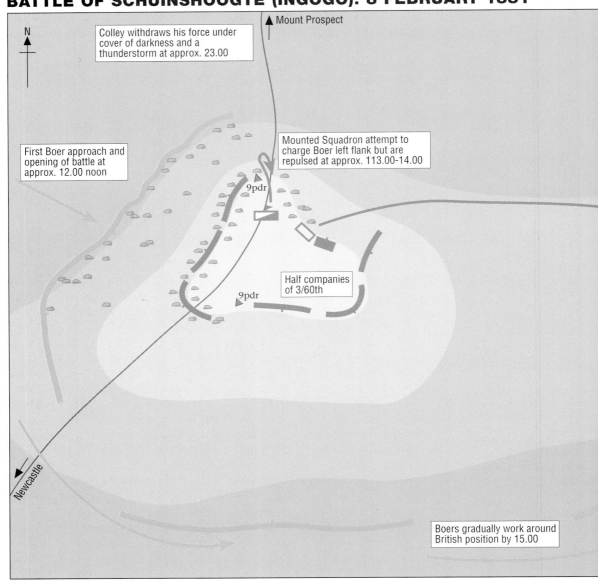

N

↑ Mount Prospect

Colley withdraws his force under cover of darkness and a thunderstorm at approx. 23.00

First Boer approach and opening of battle at approx. 12.00 noon

Mounted Squadron attempt to charge Boer left flank but are repulsed at approx. 113.00-14.00

9pdr

9pdr

Half companies of 3/60th

Newcastle

Boers gradually work around British position by 15.00

RIGHT **The cross marking the grave of Captain MacGregor, who was killed leading a half company of the 3/60th to prevent the Boers completely encircling the plateau. Beyond the graves the ground slopes down to the Ingogo, where it climbs again to Nkwelo (left) and Majuba (right).**

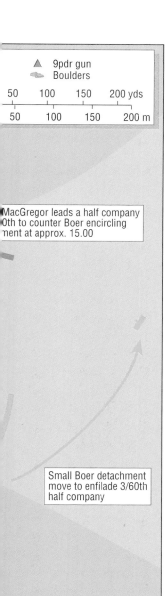

position by Colley's military secretary, Captain J.C. MacGregor, the men suffered terribly but held onto their exposed position and prevented the Boers completing their manoeuvre. Had the Boers succeeded, casualties on the plateau could have been even heavier. MacGregor, who led the men forward while still mounted, became the latest of Colley's staff to be shot dead.

There was a lull in the battle at about 3.00pm, during which Colley managed to send off a despatch to Mount Prospect. He ordered up two further companies of the 58th Regiment to join the companies of the 3/60th and 58th already in position overlooking the Ingogo river with the two 7-pdr guns.

Colley's casualties were mounting, and the situation was worsened by wounded horses galloping about the plateau in a frenzy, trampling those who could not move out of their way. It had been a hot day and the pleas for water of the wounded were pitiful; without a watercart there was nothing anyone could do to alleviate the suffering. The firing continued to flare up and die down again throughout the afternoon.

For some time the distant rumble of thunder had been audible, and just after 5.00pm the heavens opened. The parched and wretched wounded greeted the deluge with joy, as they were at last able to slake their thirst, but as the rain continued, chills set in that led to the deaths of many of these men. The light began to fade, and at 6.00pm the Boers raised a white flag. However, as Colley sent forward his chaplain to parley, firing continued on the other flank, forcing Colley to order him back. Smit, the Boer commander, tried to encourage his men to attack and bring the battle to a conclusion that night. The independent-minded Boers had learnt a lot of respect for these British who had put up such a dogged resistance during the last six hours and did not share Smit's enthusiasm in exposing themselves to British fire. It is reported that Smit's imploring was greeted with a cry of 'What the hell!'

During the latter part of the afternoon the Boers had also made attempts to threaten the detachment left overlooking the Ingogo. However, their thrust had been disturbed by the arrival of the two additional companies of the 58th Regiment which Colley had ordered up from Mount Prospect and by some good artillery practice from the two 7-pdrs and Lieutenant Parsons' 9-pdr on Schuinshoogte.

RIGHT **Colley, left, and Colonel Ashburnham, 3/60th, survey the battle from the centre of the plateau as mounting casualties are dealt with by Surgeon McGann. In the centre dead and wounded horses are cut from their traces. (Royal Greenjackets Museum, Winchester)**

HOW GEN. COLLEY RETREATED

HOW THE BOERS BEAT GEN: COLLEY: BY PICKING OFF OUR GUNNERS

52

Colley's Night March

By 7.30pm all firing on Schuinshoogte had stopped. For the next hour and a half the wounded were collected together and given what comfort was available. Colley, meanwhile, considered the difficult position he was in. He could not expect to be relieved, as there were few troops available. In addition, Mount Prospect was now very weakly defended and vulnerable to attack itself. His men were without food or water, and there would be no chance to replenish ammunition. It seemed to Colley that if he was to prevent his command being annihilated in the morning, he must march during the night. Besides, if the rain continued, the Ingogo would be too high to effect a crossing in the morning. At 9.30pm everything was ready for a daring night march. The few horses that remained standing were rounded up and attached to the two guns, and there were just enough for one of the ammunition wagons too. Those wounded unable to move were to be left on the field under the care of the Reverend Ritchie, Surgeon McGann and a civilian volunteer.

It was probably at this point that the Boers made their first critical mistake of the war. Colley sent forward a handful of scouts to discover the whereabouts of the Boers. When they eventually returned they were able to report that they had been right down to the river without finding any sign of Boer activity. With the onset of the heavy rain in the evening, Smit, who had been joined by Joubert during the day, had given the order for his men to withdraw for the night. Having pulled back to a farm about two miles away, the Boers warmed themselves by the fire, prepared food and discussed how they would finish off the hapless British at first light. They felt certain that all the horses were dead or wounded, so it would be impossible for the British to withdraw the guns across the now swollen Ingogo.

A few men, to their great disgust, were detailed to watch the drifts. One Boer source reports that their numbers had grown to 500 by sunset, and more continued to arrive during the night. The weight of Boer firepower during the fight had convinced Colley that he must have been facing 1,000 of the enemy.

Colley was eventually ready to commence his march at about 11.00pm. He formed his men into a hollow square, with the men in skirmish order and the guns in the centre. They were forbidden to make a sound, and as the square moved forward, each creak of the artillery wheels or flash of lightning spelt the end of the secret enterprise. But they were not discovered. Approaching the river by a roundabout route they encountered no Boer patrols – there were none.

Those unfortunate sentries left at the river had sought what shelter they could from the rain and saw nothing of Colley's movement. The river had risen greatly and the water now reached the soldiers' armpits. In order to cross safely the men linked arms as they struggled across, even so about seven men were drowned. Once across, the long haul up the hill began. It had been impossible in the atrocious weather conditions to locate the companies who had been left watching the river. The horses were now too weak and exhausted to pull the guns and had to be assisted

SCHUINSHOOGTE

At Schuinshoogte a British force was surrounded and pinned down by Boer fire. The infantry took cover behind the scattered boulders which lined the heights. The artillerymen were not so fortunate and suffered heavy casualties. In appalling weather volunteers from the 3/60th came forward to assist in manning the pieces.

all the way by the efforts of the 3/60th. After a superhuman effort Colley's command reached Mount Prospect at about 4.00am on the morning of 9 February. It had been a miraculous achievement.

Boer Disappointment

When Smit returned to Schuinshoogte with his commando to bring the battle to an end he was astounded to find Colley gone and no sign of the guns. The Boers searched the area, presuming that Colley had hidden the guns before retreating, even searching the river. They just could not comprehend that the guns had escaped. Back on the plateau the Boers assisted with the wounded, who were loaded onto ambulance wagons and sent on to Newcastle. A burial party formed by the Rifles returned to the battlefield later that day to help bury the dead.

British casualties had been heavy again. The 3/60th Rifles had lost 58 men killed and 63 wounded. One man had been taken prisoner. In addition one officer and seven men had drowned on the retreat or while returning to help the wounded. The artillery had lost three killed and 12 wounded as well as 14 of their 27 horses. The Mounted Squadron had suffered few casualties – three killed and two wounded – but had lost 23 of their 38 horses. Colley's personal staff again suffered: he lost Captain MacGregor and Mr Stuart, a civilian interpreter; but yet again Major Essex, the survivor of Isandlwana and Laing's Nek, confirmed his 'lucky' tag and came safely through the battle of Schuinshoogte (or Ingogo, as the British called it). Boer losses, as always, are unclear, but they are thought to be eight killed and ten wounded, of which two later died.

Nicholas Smit was angry that he had failed to inflict a crushing defeat on Colley at Schuinshoogte; he had had the opportunity but let it slip from his grasp. Colley was in no position to consider the battle anything

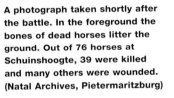

A photograph taken shortly after the battle. In the foreground the bones of dead horses litter the ground. Out of 76 horses at Schuinshoogte, 39 were killed and many others were wounded. (Natal Archives, Pietermaritzburg)

but a reverse. His demonstration in force had been surrounded and pinned down in an exposed position. Having suffered heavy casualties, he had only been able to withdraw to safety due to appalling weather conditions. With the Natal Field Force severely weakened, Colley had no choice but to remain inactive until the arrival of Evelyn Wood and the reinforcements. He deeply felt the loss of his men and staff; almost a quarter of his command had been killed or wounded since they had left Newcastle only 17 days before. In a letter to his sister, Colley confided his sadness, adding: '… Reinforcements are now arriving, and I hope it will not be long before I have force enough to terminate this hateful war.'

British Reinforcements Arrive

The first batch of reinforcements, dubbed the 'Indian Column' since all had come directly from service on the sub-continent, were ordered to form on the Biggersberg, about half-way between Ladysmith and Newcastle. This column, two squadrons of the 15th Hussars, 2/60th Rifles and 92nd Regiment, had all recently fought in the second Afghan war. They were joined by the Naval Brigade from HMS *Dido* and *Boadicea* and a few drafts for units already based at Mount Prospect. At the same time, many more reinforcements were heading for or already landing at Durban.

Evelyn Wood rendezvoused with the column on 15 February and joined the advance to Newcastle, where they were met by Colley on 17 February. Colley's plan was for Wood to take command of a column to be formed from the reinforcements on their way up and relieve Wakkerstroom and Lydenburg while Colley himself relieved Pretoria and took over the government of the Transvaal. Bellairs, who was currently besieged in Pretoria, would then be in a position to take the column on and relieve Potchefstroom and Rustenburg. Colley had added in a letter to Wood: 'You will also, I am sure, understand that I mean to take the [Laing's] Nek myself!' After discussing the current position, Wood led a reconnaissance from Newcastle on 19 February. Taking with him 100 Hussars, Wood scouted towards Wakkerstroom, probing the Boer left flank and rear. Having established that there was no large force of Boers in that area, he returned to Newcastle, having covered about 60 miles in 24 hours. On 21 February Colley inspected the Indian Column and informed them that he was proud to have such experienced soldiers under his command. He also warned them not to underestimate the Boers. The following day Colley marched with the column for Mount Prospect, having requested that Wood return to Pietermaritzburg to expedite the transportation of supplies and reinforcements to the front. There was to be no further advance until the reinforcements were in place. On 23 February the Indian Column marched into camp at Mount Prospect, but after a short halt the 2/60th were sent back to Newcastle as escort to a convoy of wagons with part of

Brevet Major Edward Essex, 75th Regiment. Having escaped from the disaster at Isandlwana during the Zulu War, he had earned the nickname 'Lucky Essex'. He certainly lived up to it in 1881, since he survived the reverses at Laing's Nek and Schuinshoogte unscathed. (Ministry of Defence)

the 15th Hussars, two troops remaining with the column. The appearance of the newly arrived 92nd Highlanders was about to change the look of warfare in southern Africa. For the first time, an Imperial unit took the field wearing khaki tunics; their officers were also equipped with the new Sam Browne belt.

Reinforcements at Mount Prospect, 23 February 1881

	Officers	Other Ranks	Total
15th Hussars	5	98	103
Royal Artillery	2	6	8
2/21st Regiment	2	7	9
58th Regiment	2	9	11
3/60th Rifles	5	21	26
92nd Regiment	17	501	518
94th Regiment	3	0	3
Army Medical Dept.	1	0	1
Naval Brigade	2	56	58
Total	39	698	737

Early Peace Negotiations

From early January, negotiations had been underway to bring about a peaceful settlement to the war. But they kept coming up against the same stumbling block: any settlement as far as the Boers were concerned would first involve the annulment of the Act of Annexation. On 12 February the Triumvirate wrote to Colley stating that they were prepared to submit their case to a Royal Commission of Inquiry if the British cancelled the annexation. If Britain refused to annul it then the Boers further stated that they would subject themselves to the will of God and fight to the last man. Colley passed the letter on to London, where it was heatedly debated. Eventually the British decided on a conditional acceptance of the Boer proposal. Colley was instructed to inform the Boers that if they ceased armed opposition he was authorised to agree an armistice prior to arrangements for a commission being made.

Colley was indignant. The government had responded rapidly to his setbacks in the Transvaal and forwarded numerous reinforcements to enable him to restore the situation. Now, with the reinforcements almost in place, Colley was ready to redress the defeats at Bronkhorstspruit, Laing's Nek and Schuinshoogte, but it appeared that the government was about to agree a compromise with the Boers. He telegraphed back to London, seeking clarification and pointing out that there could be no hostilities if the Boers did not offer resistance and adding: '... am I to leave

Mount Prospect Camp. Marked on the illustration are: (7) small defensive redoubts, (9) camps of 3/60th, (10) 58th, (11) RA, and Naval Brigade, (12) Field Hospital, (13) 92nd and 15th Hussars.

R.G.Woodville

Laing's Nek in Natal territory in Boer occupation, and our garrisons isolated and short of provisions, or occupy former and relieve latter?' In reply Colley was informed by the colonial secretary, angered by the implied criticism, that the Transvaal garrisons were to attempt to negotiate with their besiegers for provisions if the agreement proceeded, and that in the present circumstances, '... we do not mean that you should march to the relief of the garrisons or occupy Laing's Nek'. Colley was given authority to add a suitable time limit for a Boer response to the proposal; he allowed 48 hours. On 24 February the proposal was delivered to Nicholas Smit at Laing's Nek. He informed Colley that Joubert was at Heidelberg, 100 miles away, and that it would take at least four days for an answer to be forthcoming. Two days later, on 26 February, Smit forwarded the news that in fact Joubert was further away, at Rustenburg, over 200 miles distant. Joubert received the letter on 27 or 28 February and accepted the proposal, but his reply did not reach Laing's Nek until 7 March. By then it was too late.

News of Bronkhorstspruit prompted swift action in London. Reinforcements were ordered to Natal; among the first to arrive were the 92nd Highlanders direct from India. They were the first Imperial unit in Africa to wear khaki tunics. (R. England)

59

THE BATTLE OF MAJUBA

THE PLAN

Colley now pondered his next move from the camp at Mount Prospect. Ahead of him the Boers were still in position across Laing's Nek, and even appeared to be strengthening their defences. The looming presence of Majuba mountain still anchored their western flank, while the Buffalo valley provided protection to the east. In reality there was little Colley could do for the time being. He had told Wood that he would not move against the Nek until the reinforcements were in place, and he had assured the War Office that he would not undertake any operations likely to bring on an engagement while awaiting Joubert's reply. However, he had added: 'I may have to seize some ground which has hitherto been practically unoccupied by either party, lying between the Nek and our camp.' The ground he referred to was Majuba.

Amajuba in the Zulu language means the 'Hill of Doves'. To the Boers it was known as *Spitzkop*. It is now more commonly known as Majuba. The mountain rises majestically 6,000 feet above sea level and about 2,000 feet above Laing's Nek, its contours etched by ravines, ridges and cliffs. Viewed from the south, it appears to have been sliced off at the top just as it is about to come to a point.

Colley certainly did not consider his decision to occupy Majuba as an aggressive one. Majuba was in Natal, and had not been occupied by the Boers except by a few piquets in daylight hours. If he could take possession of the mountain-top during the night, there would be no need for bloodshed. Once there, he would be able to overlook the Boer defences and laagers, making their

Amajuba, the Hill of Doves. Taken from the north-west, this photo shows the mountain as seen from the Boer lines. The trees in the foreground were not present in 1881.

position below uncomfortable and perhaps inducing them to abandon the Nek. Evelyn Wood, writing 25 years later, felt Colley was justified in occupying the mountain. Throughout 26 February Colley and his replacement military secretary, Lieutenant-Colonel Herbert Stewart of the 3rd Dragoon Guards, observed Majuba through their field-glasses. Later in the day, the two interviewed a local African who had scouted the mountain. He confirmed that the Boers evacuated Majuba each night, and he described the mountain-top as a saucer-like depression ringed by boulders. Colley was also told that water could be found not far below the surface. At one point during the interview, the scout pointed towards Majuba; immediately Colley gestured to him to lower his arm. Determined to keep his plan a secret, Colley only revealed his intentions to one other person besides Stewart – Major Fraser of the Royal Engineers, another newly arrived staff officer. It had been decided: that night Majuba would be taken and that Colley himself would lead the assault.

THE NIGHT MARCH TO MAJUBA

As lights out sounded at 8.30pm and the men prepared to retire for the night, a sudden flurry of activity broke out around the staff tents. Orders were issued for two companies 58th Regiment, two companies 3/60th Rifles, three companies 92nd Highlanders, a company-strength Naval Brigade drawn from the *Boadicea* and the *Dido* as well as various small detachments from other units to be ready to march at 10.00pm. Each man was ordered to carry 70 rounds of ammunition, a greatcoat, a waterproof sheet, rations for three days and a full water bottle, along with his rifle – a total weight of 58lbs (26kg). In addition, each company was to carry four picks and six shovels. The total strength of the force as recorded by Major Essex was 595 officers and men plus Colley, Stewart and Fraser of the staff and three newspaper correspondents. There were also a number of African guides, servants and so on, but, as in all battles of this campaign, exactly how many is unrecorded.

There has been much discussion over the years as to why Colley did not take a force made up of one battalion to give greater cohesion. A number of reasons have been suggested, including the view that Colley believed his imminent capture of Majuba would prove to be the turning point of the war, and he wanted all his units to share in the glory after the earlier reverses in the campaign. This decision was to have a direct influence on what was to follow.

The route followed by Colley's force on the night of 26/27 February from the top of Majuba. In the background is Nkwelo mountain, showing the slopes up which the British marched before turning north along the connecting ridge to Majuba.

At 10.00pm the column moved off into a moonless night with no idea of its destination. The order was given for no lights to be carried and for total silence to be observed at all times. Spirits were high, and those left behind in camp envied their comrades, who were obviously off to teach the Boers a lesson. Colley and his two staff officers rode at the head of the column, following the two Zulu scouts; behind marched the 58th, 3/60th and 92nd, with the Naval Brigade bringing up the rear. They headed west from Mount Prospect, crossed the Newcastle–Laing's Nek road and proceeded to climb up the lower slopes of Nkwelo mountain. After about an hour's march they reached a plateau about half-way up and there the column reorganised itself. Next they turned north and followed a track along the side of the mountain, only wide enough for men in single file with a steep drop on one side. This path led to another open plateau at the northern end of Nkwelo, and here Colley detached the two companies of 3/60th Rifles to protect his line of march. These companies, under Captains C. Smith and R. Henley received no orders other than to hold their position, and they were not told of Colley's destination. From this plateau Colley continued his march northwards along a wide ridge which ran towards Majuba. At the far end the column halted for about an hour, around midnight, while part of the rear of the column which had lost its way in the dark was found and brought in. At this point Colley detached a company of the 92nd Highlanders, under Captain P. Robertson. His orders were to dig an entrenchment where they would be joined later by a company of 3/60th sent out from Mount Prospect. They were to be left in charge of the officers' horses, which were to proceed no further, and the reserve ammunition.

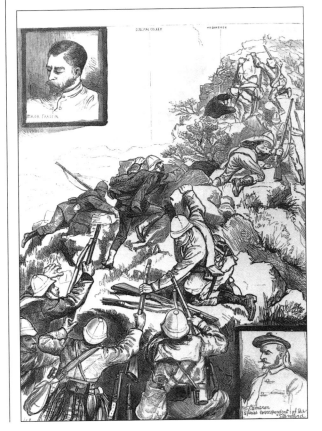

The night assault on Majuba was achieved in the most trying circumstances. It proved impossible to maintain order during the climb due to the difficult nature of the terrain. (R. England)

The Ascent of Majuba

The destination of the march was now no longer a secret. The column marched off and began to ascend the slopes of the mountain directly ahead; they were to capture Majuba. The climb was a tough one. The scouts and staff kept getting ahead of the main body, unencumbered with heavy kit as they were. Regular halts, every hundred yards, became necessary to keep the men in contact. As they clambered forward up the steeply rising track, occasionally a man would fall and clatter to the ground, which in the eerie false silence of the moment seemed to echo like a crash of thunder. Those nearby would freeze, expecting at any moment a Boer bullet to zip through the air. But they were not discovered. Close to the top the scouts lost their way in the dark, and it was a nervous time while they searched for the path again. There was only one point where they could gain the summit on this south-western angle of Majuba. Anxiously the men waited, expecting to be discovered at any moment. With the path regained, the men now faced the stiffest part of the climb. A steep grass-covered slope had to be

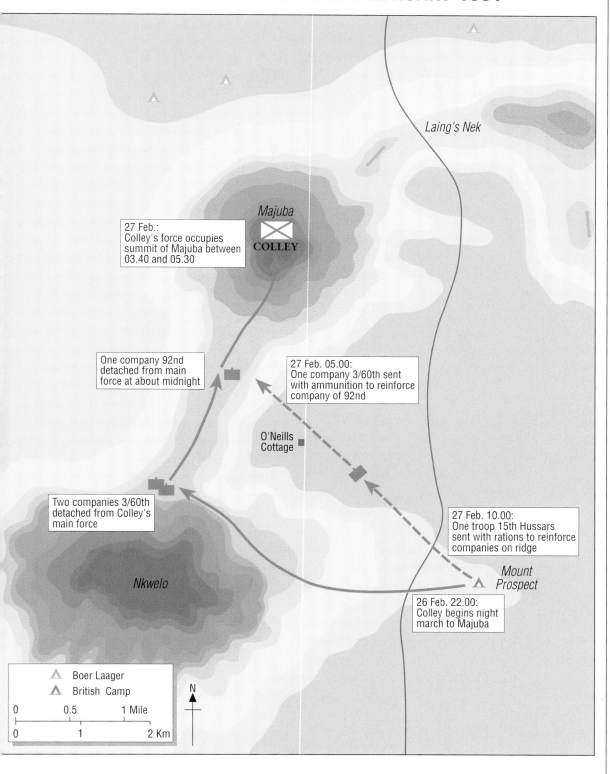

Laing's Nek

Majuba

COLLEY

27 Feb.:
Colley's force occupies
summit of Majuba between
03.40 and 05.30

One company 92nd
detached from main
force at about midnight

27 Feb. 05.00:
One company 3/60th sent
with ammunition to reinforce
company of 92nd

O'Neills
Cottage

Two companies 3/60th
detached from Colley's
main force

27 Feb. 10.00:
One troop 15th Hussars
sent with rations to reinforce
companies on ridge

Nkwelo

Mount
Prospect

26 Feb. 22.00:
Colley begins night
march to Majuba

△ Boer Laager
△ British Camp

N

0	0.5	1 Mile
0	1	2 Km

scaled. Crawling on hands and knees and pulling at tufts of grass to help them, they scrambled on. There was no longer any need to worry about the men breaking the silence order: no one had any breath to spare. The dark outline of the summit was now in sight. Colley ordered Major Fraser forward with a small detachment of the 58th to reconnoitre the mountaintop. He soon returned with the news that Colley wanted to hear. His intelligence was correct: the Boers left Majuba unoccupied at night.

Colley climbed onto the summit at 3.40am and encouraged his command forward. As the men struggled up in twos and threes, burdened with their heavy loads, Colley personally allotted the exhausted men to their positions around the summit. It was still dark, and as the difficulties of the climb had broken up the disciplined units into straggling small groups and individuals, there was some confusion when the top was gained as the men looked for their comrades. Some of the late arrivals did not actually reach their own units as they were hurried into the nearest gap in the perimeter as day began to break. The last man finally reached the summit at about 5.30am.

Occupying the Summit

As the thin light of dawn slowly illuminated the summit of Majuba it presented a pleasing aspect to Colley. Roughly triangular, the summit has a perimeter of about three quarters of a mile, lined with rough boulders, which then slopes inwards to form a basin in the centre. On the western side of the mountain is an isolated koppie, or rocky outcrop. On the eastern side there is another, although less well defined. The basin, in some places 40 feet below the perimeter of the summit, was bisected by a low rocky ridge which in the darkness was erroneously believed to mark the northern edge of the summit. Colley was heard to remark to Stewart: 'We could stay here for ever.'

British Force on Majuba Mountain, 27 February 1881

	Officers	Other Ranks	Total
Staff	3	-	3
2/21st Regiment	-	6	6
58th Regiment	7	164	171
92nd Highlanders	6	135	141
94th Regiment	2	2	4
Army Medical Dept.	2	-	2
Army Hospital Corps	-	12	12
Army Service Corps	-	1	1
Naval Brigade	3	62	65
Total	23	382	405

Boer Force on Majuba Mountain, 27 February 1881

The British occupation of Majuba had not been anticipated, so the force that attacked the mountain was assembled from volunteers from various commandos. The exact composition is unknown. Probably no more than 450 men took part in the attack, directed by Nicolas Smit.

Having told off three companies on the approach march to Majuba to protect his lines of communication, Colley's force was now reduced from 595 to 402 men. The 92nd Highlanders lined the perimeter from the koppie on the western side, later named 'MacDonald's Kop' in recognition of Lieutenant Hector MacDonald's efforts to defend it during the coming battle, along the rocky ridge to the koppie on the eastern edge, which became known as 'Hay's Kop' after Major Hay. The line was continued by the 58th along the south-eastern face to the south-western point where the force had crossed onto the summit. From here the Naval Brigade commanded the western lip up to a steep grassy gully that extended down the mountainside below MacDonald's Kop. The men were extended at roughly 12-pace intervals along the perimeter, and a mixed reserve of about 110 men was created, drawn from all three units and formed in the hollow behind the rocky ridge, close to Colley's head-quarters. The medical men also positioned themselves here and prepared a field hospital. A well was dug close by, and water was found at a depth of about three feet. Later, a second

was added. One of the newspaper correspondents, Thomas Carter of the *Natal Times*, in the relaxed atmosphere that pervaded the British position at this time, applauded this find: now they had 'something to dilute our gin with'.

Daybreak, 27 February 1881

As the skies gradually lightened it quickly became apparent that the 92nd, lining the rocky ridge, were not actually on the true perimeter of the mountain-top. Beyond the ridge which marked the actual summit the ground sloped gently away to the north before dropping abruptly to a wide flat grassy terrace below. Orders were immediately given for the 92nd to move and occupy this forward brow of Majuba, and a handful of men also took up an exposed position on an isolated featureless knoll which jutted out to the north. This feature was later known as 'Gordons' Knoll', in honour of the 92nd, who became the Gordon Highlanders later that year. The knoll was an important feature, as it enabled flanking fire to be directed across the northern slopes. At the time, no one realised just how important this position was. Having considerably extended their lines, the 92nd were now even more widely dispersed.

No serious co-ordinated effort was made to fortify the position. Colley considered the men too tired. Some have contradicted this fact, and indeed some junior officers encouraged their men to form individual defences by piling stones in front of their positions. The Naval Brigade

The surface of Majuba from the point where Colley's force reached the summit. On the left is MacDonald's Kop; extending from its foot is the rocky ridge which was at first thought to mark the northern perimeter. The highest point on the right is Hay's Kop.

Gordons' Knoll, the key to Majuba. This isolated, exposed and featureless knoll jutted out from the north-western point of Majuba. Manned by a handful of Highlanders, the position allowed flanking fire across the northern face of the mountain. Once lost, the northern perimeter became untenable.

made a serious attempt to produce some strong stone defensive positions, the remains of which are still evident today.

Colley had now achieved all his goals. Many of his officers and men now peered out towards the camp at Mount Prospect, expecting at any moment to see the force left behind march out, with the artillery, and prepare to assault Laing's Nek as part of a co-ordinated attack. But that was not Colley's plan. As has been shown earlier, Colley had been ordered by London not to capture Laing's Nek until an answer to the peace proposal had been received, and he himself had told Wood that he would not advance again until the reinforcements were in place. All he intended doing was seizing, as he had informed London, 'some ground which has hitherto been practically unoccupied by either party'. Colley felt that with their flank threatened, the Boers would probably retire, but if they did not, it was no great problem. He had already planned to hand over command on Majuba to Commander Romilly of the Naval Brigade (according to Colonel Stewart) and return to Mount Prospect to be ready for the reinforcements when they arrived from Newcastle. Then he knew the Boers, threatened from front and flank, would retire from Laing's Nek permanently and he could move to the relief of the besieged garrisons of the Transvaal. Colley has been criticised in some quarters for not taking artillery or Gatling guns up to the summit, but the steepness of the climb quite simply precludes any such action. It may have been possible to drag rocket apparatus up, but Colley did not attempt it; perhaps he intended to do so once the mountain was secure. We shall never know for sure, but what is certain is that the distance from the top of the mountain to the Boer camps below was beyond rifle range.

Now safely occupying the summit Colley considered his position almost impregnable, but he had failed to recognise one critical aspect of Majuba's topography: the slopes of the mountain on the north and north-eastern sides are

very different to those which his men had encountered on their arduous climb to the top. As has already been mentioned, a grassy slope pushed forward to the north, beyond the true summit of the mountain. But below this the ground dropped abruptly to a wide flat grass-covered terrace. Beyond this the ground again sloped sharply downwards, placing large extents of the ascent in dead ground. This, in addition to the gullies and ravines which ran down the mountain, thickly choked with bush, meant that it was possible for an attacking force to advance two-thirds of the way up the mountain virtually unseen by those lining the perimeter of the summit.

No official order had been given for the men on Majuba to construct defences. Some did pile a few rocks for protection, but Carter, the correspondent, considered that these provided poor cover and added an extra danger from bullets shattering the stones. (R. England)

THE BOER RESPONSE

In the Boer camps, of which there were three behind Laing's Nek, all was quiet. Thomas Carter, the correspondent, peered over the edge of Majuba and reported: 'Very little could we see before four o'clock; a solitary light here and there in the darkness below us. In a very short time, however, the change was marvellous; the Boer army had risen from sleep, and in every tent and wagon there was a light… It was a thrilling sight from our point of vantage; there was our enemy at our mercy, and unaware of our proximity to them.' It was a Sunday morning and the Boers were to begin their day with prayers and hymns. Discipline on the summit of Majuba was lapse, and at first light, about 4.30am, a group of Highlanders stood on the skyline shaking their fists and hurling inaudible insults towards the Boer camps below. There was no attempt to conceal the success of the night's work. Colley's men were jubilant.

The Boer commanders recognised the importance of Gordons' Knoll. Led by Commandant Ferreira, small groups of Boers began to congregate directly below the knoll, awaiting the right moment to attack the Highlanders above.

Commandant-General Joubert was in his tent writing reports when word came to him that the British were on Majuba. He rushed out to see for himself, and was astonished to see figures moving about on the top. It did not take long for word to spread through the Boer camps.

BATTLE OF MAJUBA

27 February 1881, 03.40-13.00, viewed from the north-west.
The occupation of the summit by the British and the Boer
advance.

BOER FORCES
A Boer assault group led by Commandant D.J.K. Malan
B Boer assault group led by Field Cornet S. Roos
C Boer assault group led by Commandant J. Ferreira

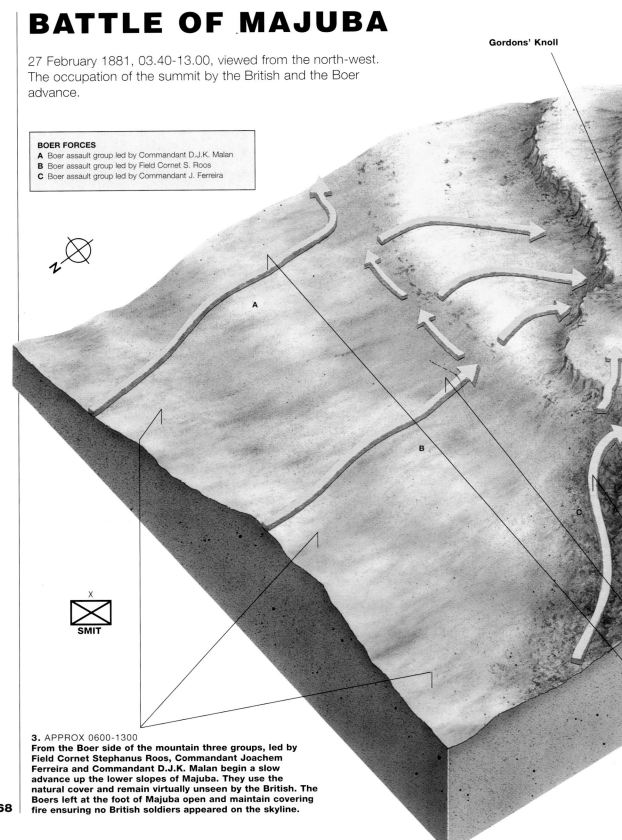

Gordons' Knoll

A

B

C

X
SMIT

3. APPROX 0600-1300
**From the Boer side of the mountain three groups, led by
Field Cornet Stephanus Roos, Commandant Joachem
Ferreira and Commandant D.J.K. Malan begin a slow
advance up the lower slopes of Majuba. They use the
natural cover and remain virtually unseen by the British. The
Boers left at the foot of Majuba open and maintain covering
fire ensuring no British soldiers appeared on the skyline.**

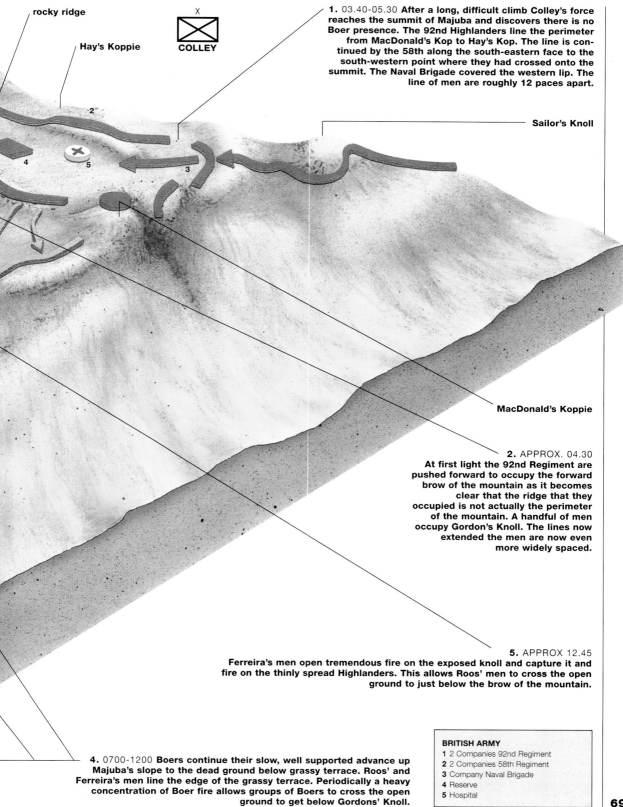

rocky ridge

Hay's Koppie

X
COLLEY

1. 03.40-05.30 **After a long, difficult climb Colley's force reaches the summit of Majuba and discovers there is no Boer presence. The 92nd Highlanders line the perimeter from MacDonald's Kop to Hay's Kop. The line is continued by the 58th along the south-eastern face to the south-western point where they had crossed onto the summit. The Naval Brigade covered the western lip. The line of men are roughly 12 paces apart.**

Sailor's Knoll

2

4   5   3

MacDonald's Koppie

2. APPROX. 04.30 **At first light the 92nd Regiment are pushed forward to occupy the forward brow of the mountain as it becomes clear that the ridge that they occupied is not actually the perimeter of the mountain. A handful of men occupy Gordon's Knoll. The lines now extended the men are now even more widely spaced.**

5. APPROX 12.45 **Ferreira's men open tremendous fire on the exposed knoll and capture it and fire on the thinly spread Highlanders. This allows Roos' men to cross the open ground to just below the brow of the mountain.**

4. 0700-1200 **Boers continue their slow, well supported advance up Majuba's slope to the dead ground below grassy terrace. Roos' and Ferreira's men line the edge of the grassy terrace. Periodically a heavy concentration of Boer fire allows groups of Boers to cross the open ground to get below Gordons' Knoll.**

BRITISH ARMY
1 2 Companies 92nd Regiment
2 2 Companies 58th Regiment
3 Company Naval Brigade
4 Reserve
5 Hospital

69

Immediately there was a rush to saddle up, inspan the wagons and prepare to depart before artillery shells fell among the tents. But the shells never came. Joubert realised: '… everything was lost to us … if they had retained possession of the hill', but when the expected bombardment did not come, and no movement was

When the Boers launched their attack on Gordons' Knoll, the mixed reserve was rushed forward, over the rocky ridge in the centre of the photo. Heavy Boer fire induced panic among the men, who broke and ran back in disorder to the ridge, where most rallied.

observed from the direction of Mount Prospect, the Boers began to rally. Joubert called a council of war. Not all the Boers had panicked at first sight of the British. A few of the more experienced individuals had galloped towards the base of the mountain and congregated there, rifles in hand. High above them Lieutenant Lucy of 58th Regiment borrowed a gun and took a shot at them at about 5.30am, although he was well out of range. Colley had not wanted any direct provocation of the Boers and immediately sent word to 'stop that firing'. The Boers opened a sporadic fire in return.

At the council of war Smit agreed with Joubert that the mountain should be retaken. As was the Boer practice, volunteers were called for by Smit to join the assault, while Joubert rode off to prepare the defences on Laing's Nek for an expected British assault. Between 50 and 80 men immediately stepped forward for the task, mounted their horses and galloped off to the lower slopes of Majuba. More men were to follow and join the attack. Smit then organised another group, about 150 strong, which rode off around the western side of the mountain with the intention of preventing any British retreat or reinforcement. The first group arrived at the base of Majuba, dismounted under cover and divided themselves into two attacking parties. Placed under the command of Field Cornet Stephanus Roos and Commandant Joachem Ferreira, the two groups began their slow, careful advance up the lower slopes of Majuba. Keeping about 100 yards apart, Roos on the left and Ferreira on the right, they took advantage of the natural cover provided by the vegetation and a large gully, and climbed virtually unseen by the British on the summit. A second group now joined the assault. Advancing to the left of Roos' men, Commandant D. Malan led forward a similar group which increased in size as those in the laagers behind Laing's Nek realised there was to be no British attack on their position. The older Boers not inclined to take an active part in the assault joined others congregated at the foot of Majuba and from about 6.00am opened a heavy covering fire which ensured that those on the summit exposed themselves against the skyline at their peril. The Boer storming parties continued their inexorable advance up the mountain, zigzagging from boulder to bush, each party providing covering fire for the other in a perfect fire and movement exercise. Targets for the British were rare, however, since most of the Boer advance so far had been over dead ground. When a target did present itself, to take aim was to present yourself as a target to the covering fire of the Boers below.

The Situation on the Summit

Back on the summit everything was calm; neither officers nor men felt any undue concern, and no-one believed for a moment that the position was anything but impregnable. Colley toured the perimeter of his position in a leisurely manner with his Staff, divulging little of his intentions to those who enquired. As the sun rose, so the air warmed, and those of the Reserve positioned in the hollow to the rear of the rocky ridge enjoyed a leisurely breakfast. While many stretched out to regain some of their hours of lost sleep, others kept an eye open for the forward movement of troops from Mount Prospect that many still presumed must commence at any moment.

At 8.00am Colley sent a signal to Mount Prospect and instructed them to telegraph it to Childers, the Secretary of State for War: 'Occupied Majuba mountain last night. Immediately overlooking Boer position. Boers firing at us from below.' At about 9.00am Colley again signalled to Mount Prospect, instructing them to order forward the 2/60th Rifles and three troops of the 15th Hussars currently stationed at Newcastle, urging them to arrive by the next morning. How Colley intended using these reinforcements is not known, but presumably he was intending to build up a force strong enough to assault Laing's Nek should hostilities re-commence once Joubert's response to the British proposals was known.

Meanwhile the level of Boer fire aimed at the summit was gradually increasing. An officer of the 58th came to the Reserve to obtain some reinforcements for his sector and had trouble waking them from their sleep. He departed with ten men.

Before he left, Carter, the correspondent, asked him if anything was wrong. The officer assured him that everything was fine but the fire was 'warming up'. Moments later the first casualty limped into the hospital area that had been set up by surgeons Landon and Mahon of the Army Medical Department. Meanwhile Colley continued his perambulations, encouraging his men and pausing to instruct Stewart to send off a reply to a signal from Mount Prospect dealing with matters of supply and reserve ammunition. Timed at 9.30am, the message added: 'All very comfortable. Boers wasting ammunition. One man wounded in foot.' Colley was described as having 'no sign of excitement or trepidation about him. Everything he did was in his usual deliberate, quiet, cool manner'.

Shortly after 10.30am Colley belatedly discussed the matter of constructing some defensive redoubts on the surface of Majuba. With his staff, Fraser and Stewart, he strolled with Commander Romilly of the Naval Brigade to the south-western point of the summit. Romilly had already been informed that he would be in command when Colley returned to Mount Prospect. While the four men stood discussing the most suitable sites for the erection of redoubts, Romilly noticed two

Once the British had retreated from the perimeter of the mountain Roos' men were able to crawl forward utilising a natural fold in the ground and get within 40 yards of the British position. This photo from the rocky ridge demonstrates the amount of cover available to the Boers.

Boers far below. The naval officer nonchalantly commented that it appeared one of the Boers was going to try and shoot them, and Colley turned to Stewart and asked him what he thought the distance was. Raising his binoculars Stewart responded that he felt it was about 900 yards. At that moment Romilly let out a cry of pain and fell to the ground by Colley's side. A bullet had entered his abdomen, smashed into his upper spine and exited through the back of his neck. It was apparent to all that the wound would probably prove fatal, but as Romilly was carried to the hospital area he said: 'I am all right.' He died three days later in camp at Mount Prospect. Colley was shattered by the event. Plans to build the redoubts were abandoned; one had been planned for this point, but Colley now considered the position to be dangerously exposed to Boer fire. From then on Colley's demeanour is reported as markedly different; he was described as 'gloomy and silent' and as having a 'grave and reserved expression'. However, he still did not appreciate the danger he was in.

The Boers were continuing their slow methodical advance up the slopes of Majuba, rarely coming into view of the British for more than a fleeting moment. Far below, behind Laing's Nek, only a handful of wagons were leaving the laagers. The Boers were now determined to take Majuba. But for Colley everything still appeared to be going to plan. At 11.00am he ordered another signal to be made to Mount Prospect instructing them to forward the information to Childers in London. The telegraph stated: 'Boers still firing heavily on hill, but have broken up laager and begin to move away. I regret to say Commander Romilly dangerously wounded; other casualties three men slightly wounded.'

BELOW **Although rather too crowded and heroic, this picture reflects the confusion behind the rocky ridge. Highlanders, Naval Brigade and men of the 58th intermingle as the Boers begin to close in. Colley stands centre left directing his men.**

The Boer Concentration Below Gordons' Knoll

The most northerly point of the British defensive perimeter was occupied by about 18 men of the 92nd Highlanders, under the command of Lieutenant Ian Hamilton (later General Sir Ian Hamilton who led the Gallipoli landings in 1915). He had pushed forward about five of his men to occupy the isolated knoll (later known

as 'Gordons' Knoll') and the spur that connected it with the summit. Directly below the knoll the wide flat grassy terrace narrowed dramatically. The importance of this feature was soon grasped by the leaders of the Boer assault parties, and a group, under Commandant Ferreira, began to congregate below the brow of the terrace at this narrowest point. The edge of the terrace marked the end of the dead ground, so any further Boer advance would be in the open, fully exposed to the fire of the British lining the perimeter of the summit and the knoll. Field Cornet Roos' men extended to the left of Ferreira, lining the edge of the terrace as it opened out to its full width. As more men arrived and took up their positions, so the Boer fire increased; every now and again a particularly heavy concentration of fire would be directed at the Highlanders, forcing them to keep their heads down. Taking advantage of this, groups of ten or 15 Boers would dash across the 20 yards of narrow terrace below the knoll and again disappear from view. Hamilton was powerless to stop this build-up of men dangerously close to his position, and when he estimated that as many as 100 were hidden below him he ran the gauntlet of Boer fire to report the situation to Colley, who he found in the central hollow behind the rocky ridge.

Hamilton could not help but notice how different the situation was here. Away from the Boer fire that was causing him such concern, he found the reserve 'very comfortably eating, sleeping or smoking'. Colley thanked Hamilton for the information and sent him back to his men. He took no action. Back on the perimeter Hamilton noted that the Boer strength all along the edge of the terrace was growing. When he estimated that Boer numbers had grown to 200, he reported back to Colley, who still appeared unconcerned. Becoming desperate, Hamilton again informed Colley when he felt there were 350 men building up and begged for reinforcements to help him keep the enemy fire down. Eventually Hamilton received five men and an officer of the 58th Regiment as his reinforcement.

At about midday Thomas Carter managed to send off a telegram for his newspaper. In it, full of confidence, he informed his readers: 'Firing kept up incessantly by Boers – our men very steady, return fire only when good chance offers …Boers cannot take position from us … they are keeping up average of sixty shots per minute … the Boers have inspanned their cattle and are evidently ready to trek at a moment's notice.' But within the next 90 minutes Majuba was to become the scene of one of the British Army's most humiliating defeats.

Shortly after noon Hamilton returned once more to the centre of the summit, 'feeling uneasy', to make Colley aware that he

now believed 400 Boers were extended below him and might be preparing to attack. Hamilton, with great concern for the safety of the position, must have been rather shaken to hear that Colley was actually asleep, and it appears that Stewart declined to waken him. No doubt bewildered and exasperated, Lieutenant Hamilton reported to his senior officer, Major Hay, before returning to his men on the perimeter.

The Attack on Gordons' Knoll

At about this time, between 12.30pm and 12.45pm, Carter, having sent off his despatch and finished his lunch, was engaged in conversation with another officer of the 92nd. As they spoke there was a sudden outburst of firing. Carter noted that it struck him as unusual since all the Boer fire so far had been in single shots, but this now was most definitely a volley, and it appeared to be concentrated on one point; furthermore, it appeared to be rather close.

Back on the slopes of Majuba the Boers had not been idle. Commandant Ferreira had collected between 60 and 80 men directly below Gordons' Knoll, out of sight of the Highlanders. They had been carefully watching the actions of the men on the knoll and its connecting spur. When everyone was in position, a signal was given and the Boers stepped out from their cover and opened a tremendous fire on the exposed position. The bullets, flying thick and fast, swept across the promontory. Three men were killed instantly; the other two fled for their lives back towards Hamilton and the perimeter. This was the volley that had interrupted Carter's conversation; it also awoke Colley. Ferreira's men took position of the now abandoned knoll, just 70 yards from the perimeter of the mountain, and began to open an even more galling fire on the thinly spread Highlanders. With the British now so effectively pinned down, Roos was able to lead his men in a dash across the grassy terrace to the dead ground just 100 yards below the brow of the mountain. From here only a stiff climb up the steepest part of the north face separated him from the British. The Highlanders could do nothing to oppose this move; to lean over the brow of the mountain and fire down was to present a clear target to the Boer marksmen on the knoll.

The Collapse of the Northern Perimeter

The startling volley had finally stung those in command into action. Colonel Stewart, who had been towards the south side of the summit, came running into the centre with two or three officers and ordered the greater part of the Reserve to reinforce the threatened position on the northern perimeter. The Reserve, shaken from their torpor by the peremptory shouts of the officers, grabbed their weapons and equipment amid the confusion and bewilderment. The officers had to make great efforts to encourage the men forward as they crossed the rocky ridge

Colley, revolver in hand, received news that his right flank was threatened. He ordered Hay's Kop to be held at all costs. Moments later 'a sudden piercing cry of terror' broke out from the line and the position crumbled.

and advanced in skirmishing order. Hamilton watched the Reserve come forward and noticed that it consisted of 'bluejackets, 58th and ten men of ours. They had fixed cutlasses and bayonets, and I fancied by their manner that they must have been startled by being so suddenly hurried up – anyway I did not much like the way they came up.' The Reserve quickly lay down in the grass and opened a heavy random fire, without really being able to pick out targets.

After a few minutes the Boer firing ceased, causing the officers with the Reserve to call a halt to the British fire. No Boers could be seen. There was a brief uneasy silence then the Boer fire from the knoll resumed with terrible intensity. At about the same moment, Roos and about 50 men, who had clambered up the steep final approach to the summit, were positioned on the perimeter of the mountain, just below the brow and only yards from the Highlanders. Within moments of the Boers reopening fire, about 16 of the Reserve were shot. Roos, clinging nervously to the side of the mountain, feared a bayonet charge at any moment which would sweep his men off the mountain. To encourage his men he falsely told them that the British were running. Encouraged by this, a few of his men pushed their rifles tentatively over the brow and joined the firefight.

The Reserve had seen enough. They turned and rushed back towards the rocky ridge. Those of Hamilton's men still in position joined them. The Boers were on the outer summit of the mountain and shooting the panicking British as they retreated. Hamilton made it to the rocky ridge, but few of his men were so lucky. The fleeing men crossed the rocky ridge in total disorder and appeared to be heading towards the south side of the summit, that nearest to Mount Prospect, before the majority were rallied and brought back to the ridge. They clustered towards the left or western end of the ridge while the officers attempted to separate the breathless men back into their units and extend them along the ridge. Colley was here, close to his men, looking 'cool and collected'. While this reorganisation was taking place, there was a lull in the Boer firing as they too consolidated their position on the mountain prior to the next phase of their attack.

With the collapse of the line it was every man for himself. The Boers swarmed up onto the summit and opened a heavy fire on the fleeing British. At the southern perimeter, shown here, the men threw themselves over the edge of the mountain and trusted to luck for survival. (I. Knight)

The Boers Close In

Colley's force now occupied the original line they had taken up during the night, which was still a fairly strong position. The front was now the line of the rocky ridge, which offered good cover; to the left the eminence of MacDonald's Kop, occupied by Lieutenant MacDonald and a few men, could provide covering fire and threaten any Boer moves against the front. The rear of the rocky ridge was protected by the men on Hay's Kop, and around the remainder of the perimeter were many men who had yet to fire a shot. But the weakness of the position was now in the morale of the men. The confidence of early morning had been replaced by fear, confusion and nervousness. Men positioned on the perimeter of the mountain away from the Boer attack had no idea what was happening. Widely spread and away from the direct influence of their officers, many of them, aware of the sudden build-up of men behind the ridge, grew nervous. A few began to quit their posts, under a variety of excuses, and converge on the ridge, weakening the already extended perimeter defences.

The Boers now opened a heavy fire against the rocky ridge from the front. Having crept forward to a distance of about 40 yards, taking advantage of a fold in the ground, they were keeping up a largely random fire against the ridge, designed to keep the British heads down. All that could be seen of the Boers was the odd rifle barrel jutting through the grass and smoke as another bullet splattered against the rocks on the

MACDONALD'S KOP
When the main British position collapsed Lieutenant MacDonald, 92nd Highlanders, gathered a group of about 20 men together on the high point of the mountain, later known as MacDonald's Kop. They held out until only MacDonald and one other man remained unscathed, their surrender ending the last organised resistance on Majuba.

ridge. Bullets that flew too high fell among the defenders of Hay's Kop to the rear. MacDonald's men, on the Kop to the left of the ridge, were unable to restrict this fire as they were themselves pinned down by fire from the knoll captured earlier. More worryingly, a group of Ferreira's men were advancing around the west of the mountain, just below them, moving towards the gully behind their position that led up to the summit. To make matters even worse, Commandant Malan, who had begun his climb after Roos and Ferreira, had worked his way around the mountain to the east and was now firing up at the men of the 58th defending Hay's Kop who were also receiving fire in their rear (described above). The Boers were closing in for the kill on three sides simultaneously; time was running out for Colley.

ABOVE **The rout. Those British who were not injured as they careered down the mountain became easy targets for the Boers now lining the edge of the mountain, who likened it to shooting game.**

Waring

Those who survived the retreat eventually struggled back to camp. One laconically described his experiences of the day; it had taken him five hours to climb the mountain but he only touched it three times on the way down. (I. Knight)

British Preparations for a Boer Assault

Once the troops behind the ridge had been shaken into the best order possible, a command rang out: 'Fix bayonets!' Words of encouragement from the staff officers cut through the increasing din, and Thomas Carter, sheltering only a few yards away, was reassured by this action. He felt it would be only a few minutes before the men stormed forward into the hail of bullets and drove the Boers from the mountain. In the meantime the wayward exchange of rifle fire continued. Towards the right of the line, Lieutenant Hamilton was preparing for action of his own. Gathering a few men of the 92nd, although heavily outnumbered, he was preparing a charge but was prevented by Major Hay, who pointed out the weakness of the group.

Undaunted, Hamilton determined to press his cause and ran to Colley, saluted and appealed: 'I do hope, General, that you will let us have a charge, and that you will not think it presumption on my part to have come up and asked you.' Colley, maintaining his calm dignity replied: 'No presumption, Mr Hamilton, but we will wait until the Boers advance on us, then give them a volley and charge.' Having failed to secure the permission he sought Hamilton reluctantly returned to his position. In the post-battle analysis those who had been present on the mountain offered varying opinions as to the potential success or failure of a bayonet charge; however, none was ever ordered.

THE COLLAPSE OF THE BRITISH POSITION

Casualties were slowly mounting as the wounded limped, crawled or were carried to the makeshift hospital, where the surgeons quickly bandaged them up and sent those fit enough back to the firing line. A new crisis now faced the defenders on the summit. Word was brought to the ridge by members of the Naval Brigade manning the south-western lip that the Boers (Ferreira's men) were moving up the large gully on the western side. This gully opened out to the left rear of the rocky ridge and would have presented the Boers with the opportunity of very close-range fire into the flank of the main British position. Orders were given for men to extend about 20 yards to the left to prevent the threatened incursion, but this meant leaving the protection of the rocky ridge.

The scene that followed was described by Carter as one of 'wild excitement'. The men nearest this point were a mixed bunch – men of the 92nd, 58th and sailors – and they showed a great unwillingness to leave cover and follow officers that were not necessarily their own. Stewart and Fraser joined the regimental officers in urging the men to the new position by a small bush; in twos and threes some reluctantly edged forward, flat on their stomachs. Others could not be moved. As Carter succinctly put it: 'Discipline was on the wane.'

Now more men, confused by the turn of events, began to leave their allotted positions around the perimeter and gathered at the rocky ridge. An officer was positioned to prevent this weakening of the overall position, but as he interrogated one small group of two or three men as to their purpose another would slip by and join the main group pinned down behind the ridge, adding to the growing confusion. Major Hay then informed Colley, who was pacing up and down with his revolver drawn, that the Boers were pressing against the kop (which would later bear his name). From here, the rear of the British position at the ridge would be completely exposed. Colley instructed the officer on the kop to hold his position at all costs and began to direct some men to extend to the right.

At that moment 'a sudden piercing cry of terror' burst forth, possibly from the group detailed to oppose the Boer attack up the gully. Men were seen in twos and threes making for the line of retreat. The men positioned behind the ridge stopped firing and turned around, panic was setting in. Four or five men broke ranks and started to run for the rear. Officers shouted after the men that they would shoot if they did not return. Seven or eight more began to run.

Another 'despairing cry' was heard, and the whole line collapsed, each man sprinting for his life. Lieutenant Hamilton had just spotted a Boer lying in the grass only 15 yards from his own position. As he took aim with a rifle he had picked up, the Boer fired and hit Hamilton in the wrist. Hamilton fell to the ground, turned to face the rear and saw that the whole line had just given way. He says he saw Colley standing with his revolver held above his head shouting that the men should hold by the ridge that marked the south-western face of the mountain, which was across the line of retreat. Hamilton then joined the rout. In an instant Boers appeared on Hay's Kop and on the rocky ridge, and opened a lethal fire on the retreating infantry. For the Boer marksmen this was easy sport, they likened it to shooting buck or pigeons. But the firing was indiscriminate.

In the hospital area Lance-Corporal Farmer of the Army Hospital Corps was standing over Surgeon Landon, who was badly wounded. Holding a bandage aloft to indicate the presence of wounded men, Farmer was immediately shot in the right wrist. Undaunted, he shouted: 'I have got another,' picked up the bandage and waved it in his other hand. This time a bullet smashed into his left elbow and he collapsed to the ground in agony. Farmer received the Victoria Cross for his selfless courage.

There was no attempt to make a stand at the far end of the mountain, the fugitives just threw themselves over the steep edge, trusting to luck

The last resistance on Majuba was offered by Lieutenant Hector MacDonald. Captured on the summit, MacDonald laid into the Boers with kicks and punches. His life was saved by one of his victims who said such a brave man should not be shot. MacDonald, who had enlisted as a private, remarkably rose to the rank of Major-General.

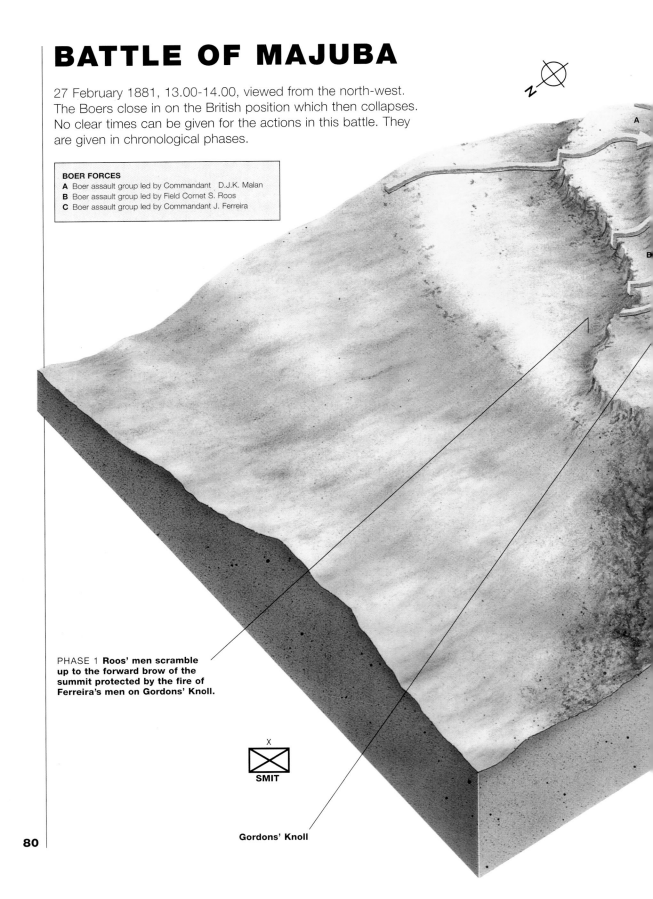

BATTLE OF MAJUBA

27 February 1881, 13.00-14.00, viewed from the north-west.
The Boers close in on the British position which then collapses.
No clear times can be given for the actions in this battle. They
are given in chronological phases.

BOER FORCES
A Boer assault group led by Commandant D.J.K. Malan
B Boer assault group led by Field Cornet S. Roos
C Boer assault group led by Commandant J. Ferreira

PHASE 1 **Roos' men scramble
up to the forward brow of the
summit protected by the fire of
Ferreira's men on Gordons' Knoll.**

X

SMIT

Gordons' Knoll

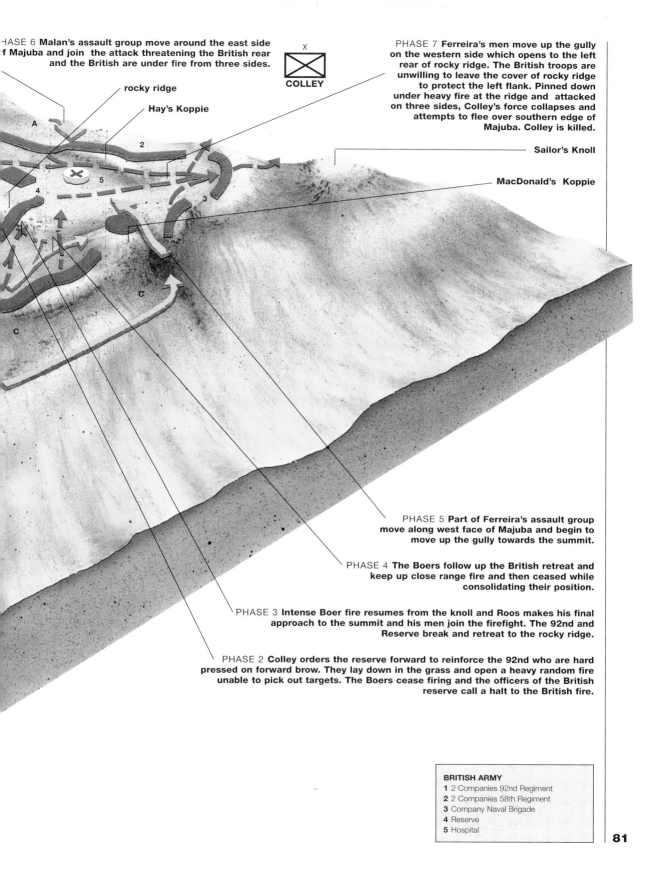

HASE 6 **Malan's assault group move around the east side f Majuba and join the attack threatening the British rear and the British are under fire from three sides.**

PHASE 7 **Ferreira's men move up the gully on the western side which opens to the left rear of rocky ridge. The British troops are unwilling to leave the cover of rocky ridge to protect the left flank. Pinned down under heavy fire at the ridge and attacked on three sides, Colley's force collapses and attempts to flee over southern edge of Majuba. Colley is killed.**

X
COLLEY

rocky ridge

Hay's Koppie

Sailor's Knoll

MacDonald's Koppie

A

2

5

4

3

C

C

PHASE 5 **Part of Ferreira's assault group move along west face of Majuba and begin to move up the gully towards the summit.**

PHASE 4 **The Boers follow up the British retreat and keep up close range fire and then ceased while consolidating their position.**

PHASE 3 **Intense Boer fire resumes from the knoll and Roos makes his final approach to the summit and his men join the firefight. The 92nd and Reserve break and retreat to the rocky ridge.**

PHASE 2 **Colley orders the reserve forward to reinforce the 92nd who are hard pressed on forward brow. They lay down in the grass and open a heavy random fire unable to pick out targets. The Boers cease firing and the officers of the British reserve call a halt to the British fire.**

BRITISH ARMY
1 2 Companies 92nd Regiment
2 2 Companies 58th Regiment
3 Company Naval Brigade
4 Reserve
5 Hospital

for survival among the rocks, precipices and gullies on the slopes of Majuba. The last resistance on the mountain appears to have been offered by Lieutenant MacDonald who gathered a group of 20 men on the western kop as the line began to break. Of this group eight were soon dead and three wounded, but he determined to hold his position, believing that the main group would rally. When they did not, MacDonald ordered his men to retire as best they could. All were shot except MacDonald and one other man, and both were taken prisoner. In a little over 30 minutes, starting with the Boer attack on Gordons' Knoll, Colley's force had been swept off the 'unassailable' and 'impregnable' mountain-top.

The Death of Colley

There are a number of accounts detailing Colley's last moments, but it still not clear exactly how he met his end. What is certain is that he was shot in the head and would appear to have died instantly. Whether he was moving to rally his command, walking towards the Boers with a white handkerchief tied to his sword or retiring will always remain rather uncertain. Some reports say he was shot at close range by a 12-year-old boy; others say he was shot at longer range by one of a group consisting of Roos, Ferreira and two other men. From the confusion of a military disaster, it can prove difficult to extract the facts.

Return to Mount Prospect

Perhaps as few as 450 Boers had taken part in the storming of Majuba. Once on the summit, the Boers looted the dead and wounded before gathering at the most southerly point of the mountain and opening a heavy fire on the fleeing British, who were scrambling for safety. Below the mountain the company of the 92nd that had been left on the approach march had been reinforced by a company of the 3/60th and a troop of the 15th Hussars during the day. These men prepared to hold their position for as long as possible, and brought in some of the first refugees to come down the mountain. But just as pressure was mounting from the group of Boers that had ridden around the western side of the mountain at the onset of the battle and another group on foot already closing on the position, an order for withdrawal was received from Mount Prospect. This was achieved in the most difficult of circumstances.

More survivors gradually struggled into Mount Prospect, many bearing horrific wounds, each with his own tale of terror to relate.

When all the information from the survivors had been collated and the bodies of the men buried, the true scale of the

The spot where Colley was killed. This small walled enclosure lies behind the rocky ridge, which can be seen extending away towards the horizon. Accounts of Colley's last moments are contradictory.

disaster became known and was passed on to a stunned and incredulous public at home. The losses, which include killed, wounded, prisoners and missing amounted to 240 men (59 per cent of the total force engaged on the mountain-top). The 92nd suffered most with a loss of 99 men (70 per cent of those in action). In stark contrast, the success of the Boer tactics is unequivocally demonstrated in their casualty figures. The Boers lost only one man killed and six wounded, one of whom later died. Those who had captured firearms claimed that many of the British guns were still sighted at 400 yards, even though much of the firing later in the battle had been at very close range. It had been a crushing defeat, and one the Army was determined to avenge.

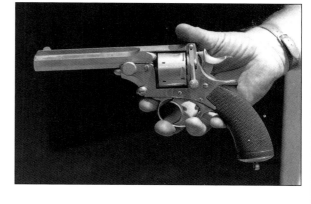

The revolver used by Colley at Majuba. This .45 Holland and Holland weapon was taken from Colley's body and remained in the possession of Joubert's family for almost a century before being donated to the museum at Fort Klapperkop, Pretoria. (M. Boswell)

British Losses at Majuba, 27 February 1881

Officers

	Killed	Wounded	Prisoners	Total	% of engaged
Staff	1	-	1	2	66
58th Regiment	1	3	1	5	71
92nd Regiment	-	3	3	6	100
94th Regiment	-	1	1	2	100
Army Medical Dept.	1	-	-	1	50
Naval Brigade	1	1	-	2	66
Total	4	8	6	18	78

Other Ranks

	Kill.	Wound.	Pris.	Missing	Total	% of engaged
2/21st Regiment	2	-	-	-	2	33
58th Regiment	31	42	13	2	88	54
92nd Regiment	31	51	11	-	93	69
94th Regiment	1	1	-	-	2	100
Army Hosp. Corps	-	2	-	-	2	16
Naval Brigade	16	15	3	-	34	55
Total	81	111	27	2	221	58

A further 43 losses were encountered in the defensive action on the ridge below Majuba.

	Officers		Other Ranks			
	Kill.	Pris.	Kill.	Wound.	Pris.	Total
15th Hussars	-	-	2	1	1	4
3/60th Rifles	-	-	-	1	11	12
92nd Regiment	-	1	4	10	10	25
Army Med. Dept	1	-	-	-	-	1
Army Service Corps	-	-	-	-	1	1
Total	1	1	6	12	23	43

LANCE CORPORAL FARMER'S COURAGEOUS ACT

With the collapse of the line the Hospital position found itself hopelessly exposed. With an unselfish display of courage Lance Corporal Farmer of the Army Hospital Corps was wounded twice while attempting to indicate that there were wounded men present. For his bravery Farmer was awarded the Victoria Cross.

THE AFTERMATH

When the news of the latest disaster broke in London, the following day, there was a feeling of outrage and a determination to exact redress before peace talks could continue. Orders were immediately issued for six infantry battalions and three cavalry regiments to embark for Natal, and Sir Frederick Roberts was appointed to replace Colley. In Natal Sir Evelyn Wood was quickly sworn in as acting Governor of Natal and High Commissioner of the Transvaal. On 4 March Wood received a communication from Joubert offering a meeting two days later. Following advice from London, Wood went ahead with the meeting and agreed to an eight-day truce; as far as he was concerned this

A sketch of the end of the Battle of Majuba from a hill above Mount Prospect camp. The Boers in possession of the summit are firing down at the British while other groups are moving around the hill attempting to cut off their retreat. (R. England)

1.___ Enemy coming round hill to attack retreating party.
2.___ Enemy in possession of Majuba Mountain doing d? d?
3.___ Enemy in Dongas & side of hill .... d? d?
4.___ Our troops retreating down side of hill under heavy fire.
5.___ Shell fired from Mount Prospect Camp, about 3m. distant.
6.___ Ledge of rocks
7.___ Hussars Picket & some officers of 60th Rifles & others looking on at the Battle.
8.___ 15th Hussars retreating.
9.___ Falls (small.)
10.___ Laing's Neck.

would give him enough time to prepare his forces for a continuation of the conflict. On 7 March Kruger's reply to Colley's letter that had been delivered into Smit's hands on 24 February was received. Wood was concerned; the reply was far more conciliatory than had been expected and could offer a chance of peace. The Army was not yet ready for peace.

Gladstone, the British prime minister, was in favour of negotiations, feeling that to shed more blood to regain prestige was wrong. It was a brave decision; even the Queen was in favour of a continuation of the war until a victory had been gained. Wood was instructed to open peace talks, distasteful as he found the proceedings. Finally, on 23 March, the formal peace agreement was signed. Roberts and the reinforcements were telegraphed to return to England. All the stalwart British garrisons in the Transvaal had held out except Potchefstroom, which eventually capitulated on 23 March, 17 days after the first truce was agreed due to Boer duplicity. The agreement was eventually ratified in August, granting a quasi-independence to the Transvaal. The Army was outraged. Carter, who was still filing copy for his newspaper, regarded it as 'a miserable ending to a miserable war'. The clauses, when made public, caused great consternation, particularly among the Boers. But Joubert was a clever man. He felt sure that once the British had confirmed the cease-fire they would not return to war; then there would be time to modify the terms in their favour. Joubert was right: three years later the Transvaal regained its full independence at the Convention of London.

The might of the British Empire had been defeated by a small infant republic with no standing army. The victory at Majuba became enshrined in Boer folk history. Alongside the Great Trek it served as a great source of inspiration and a symbol of unity for the next generations. For the British, this humiliating defeat continued to rankle; when 18 years later war with the Boers broke out again, the British Army went into battle burning with the desire for revenge and with the cry 'Remember Majuba!' on their lips. On 27 February 1900, the 19th anniversary of the battle, Lord Roberts forced the surrender of the Boer general Piet Cronje and 4,000 of his men at Paardeberg. Roberts had been urged to make the final telling attack on this day by General Hector MacDonald, survivor of Majuba. At the surrender, Cronje is reported to have lamented: 'You have even taken our Majuba day away from us.'

On 6 March a meeting was arranged midway between the lines. The Boer delegation was led by Piet Joubert (third from left), the British by Evelyn Wood (third from right). An eight-day armistice was agreed.

THE BATTLEFIELDS TODAY

One of the great advantages to a researcher interested in the battles of South Africa is the condition of the battlefields. It is over 100 years since the dramatic conflicts of the First Anglo-Boer war passed into the pages of history, but it is still possible to stand where that history was made, on ground largely unaltered by the progress of time.

As at the time of the war, the ideal base for exploring these battlefields is the northern Natal town of Newcastle. From here it is but a short drive to Laing's Nek, Schuinshoogte and Majuba. Of the three, the

Much to the disgust of the Army, a peace agreement was reached on 21 March. The meeting, which is depicted here, took place at O'Neill's farmhouse, below Majuba. The treaty was formally signed two days later.

easiest to survey is Schuinshoogte. By approaching on the main Newcastle-Volksrust road, turning off at the Ingogo sign and turning again across the double drift onto the Memel Road, you find yourself following Colley's route up onto the lonely heights. Here the monuments and graves bear silent testimony to the lives of those that were lost.

Before tackling Laing's Nek it is worth visiting the offices of the Newcastle Publicity Association (NPA). Laing's Nek and the cemetery at Mount Prospect, which contains 51 graves of officers and men killed during the war, are on private land. The NPA can arrange local guides to overcome this problem. If not, an overall view of the Laing's Nek battlefield can be gained from a roadside picnic area. Much of Laing's Nek is today covered by the trees of Majuba Forestry, but the climb up the spur undertaken by the 58th Regiment will still take your breath away. The mass graves that loom from clearings in the trees bring home the futility of the attack.

Majuba, like Isandlwana, the scene of that other great British defeat, has a brooding character all of its own. From a picnic area at the foot of Majuba, a pathway to the summit follows the Boer advance. The dead ground becomes obvious. Once on the top, you can appreciate the dominating presence of the mountain and imagine some of the feelings of the British who looked on the Boer positions far below on that fateful morning. A monument has been erected on MacDonald's Kop by descendants of the Boers, while the graves of the British lie undisturbed on the windswept summit. A few steps away is a small walled enclosure containing a weather-beaten white cross which bears the simple inscription 'This marks the spot where Gen. Colley fell.' Pause for a moment and let your mind conjure up images of this tragic struggle, for here Major–General Sir George Pomeroy-Colley found his hill of destiny.

CHRONOLOGY

1877

12 April — Britain annexes the Transvaal.

1879

Jan - Jul — Anglo-Zulu War.

3 March — Sir Owen Lanyon appointed Transvaal Administrator.

23 June — Sir Garnet Wolseley arrives to take up post as High Commissioner.

1880

April — Wolseley returns to England and is replaced by Sir George Pomeroy-Colley.

11 Nov — The Bezuidenhout affair.

16 Dec — Transvaal formally declares independence.

16 Dec. — Shots fired at Potchefstroom.

20 Dec — The action at Bronkhorstspruit.

22 Dec - 6 Jan — British garrisons in Transvaal become besieged.

1881

1 Jan — Boers form a laager at Coldstream just inside the Natal border.

19 Jan — Natal Field Force (NFF) assembles at Newcastle.

25 Jan — First British reinforcements arrive at Durban.

26 Jan — NFF forms camp at Mount Prospect.

26 Jan — Boers establish themselves on Laing's Nek.

28 Jan — Battle of Laing's Nek.

8 Feb — Battle of Schuinshoogte (Ingogo).

17 Feb — Evelyn Wood arrives at Newcastle with first reinforcements (Indian Column).

23 Feb — Indian Column arrives at Mount Prospect.

27 Feb — Battle of Majuba.

6 March — Truce agreed.

23 March — Formal peace agreement signed.

A GUIDE TO FURTHER READING

The Boers greeting the news of peace in the laagers behind Laing's Nek. Later there was a thanksgiving service. Some Boers departed for home that night. In the British camp the morale of the officers and men was shattered by the treaty.

The grave of Sir George Pomeroy-Colley in the cemetery at Mount Prospect. The graves are some distance from the road and on private land, so it is advisable to contact the Newcastle Publicity Association to arrange a visit.

Bellairs, Lady B., *The Transvaal War 1880-1881*, Edinburgh and London 1885 (reprinted Cape Town, 1972). Concentrates mainly on the besieged garrisons but also reprints many of the documents concerned with the armistice.

Butterfield, Dr P.H., *War and Peace in South Africa 1879-1881*, Melville, S.A. 1986. The letters of Brevet Lieutenant-Colonel P. Anstruther, 94th Regiment, who was mortally wounded at Bronkhorstspruit and the *Journal of the Natal Field Force* compiled by Brevet Major E. Essex. Invaluable.

Carter, T.F., *A Narrative of the Boer War*, Cape Town 1896 and London 1900. Without doubt the best first-hand account of the war. Carter was present at Schuinshoogte and Majuba as a correspondent. Most later accounts have relied heavily on this work.

Lehmann, J. , *The First Boer War*, London 1972. The most readily available account as it has recently been republished in paperback. Generally good, but perhaps the weakest part of the book is the chapter on Majuba; the map of the battle is inaccurate, and some photos have been wrongly captioned.

Norris-Newman, C.L, *With the Boers in the Transvaal and Orange Free State 1880-1881*, London 1882 (reprinted Johannesburg 1976). The author arrived too late to witness the war at first hand, but brought together the accounts of correspondents and official despatches from both sides to compile his history. He was present during the peace negotiations.

Ransford, O., *The Battle of Majuba Hill*, London 1967. A good account, although relatively short; regularly appears on the lists of military book-dealers.

WARGAMING MAJUBA

The Transvaal War is a visually attractive, and apparently straightforward wargames period, the last occasion British troops fought in rifle green and red, or carried their regimental colours in action. The forces were small, fighting over battlefields only a few thousand yards across, that are easily represented on the tabletop.

However this simplicity is deceptive. The Transvaal War was in fact a complex, transitional period, fought by quite different military systems, and providing a devastating demonstration of the effects of modern fire and movement. Consequently it presents a unique set of problems to the wargamer, demanding a specific, customised approach. This uniqueness makes it unlikely that generalised commercial wargame rules will be appropriate, any more than 19th century tactical manuals could lay down a standard approach for the ever varied opponents the British Army might have to confront.

The consistently one-sided results of the fighting in the Transvaal raises the question of how far wargames should be played to win, and how far to recreate the historical outcome. Usually the ability of the players determines the quality of tabletop command. In the Transvaal so many basic mistakes were made that the British side's freedom of action must be limited to reflect this. For example, use dice:
- to control the 58th's deployment from company column at Laing's Nek
- to dig in at Majuba
- to prevent the mounted troops prematurely charging any Boers within 1000 yards.

More difficult to represent is the over-confidence of the British command in the opening actions, which demands a concealed scenario. For example, until the farmers turn out to have rifles instead of pikes, Laing's Nek could masquerade as an action from the 1798 Troubles in Ireland, to which Colley's tactics and attitudes might have been more appropriate.

OPPOSING FORCES

These were very different. The Boers were amateurs whose individual skills allowed them to reverse the situation usual in colonial wars, inflicting the sort of loss ratio on the British that they usually imposed upon their spear armed opponents. However, the Boers would not throw their lives away by advancing under aimed fire, any more than they would hold a position once outflanked. The British, on the other hand, fielded a very conventional force, moving in a predictable and visible manner. Although their regiments were a mix of short and long service units, there was effectively little difference between them other than dress. Even the Navy's Field Exercise training was modelled closely on the Army's. Unlike the Boers however, British units could suffer heavy casualties, in the order of a third to a half, without their morale collapsing, at least until the final débâcle. The unusually high proportion of British dead shows how far ahead the Boers were in field craft and marksmanship: the farmers shot to kill, while the British could not even see them.

It is essential therefore that, in a two-sided game, the Boers' numbers and position should not be too obvious. However, as they used black powder, it is reasonable to place some Boer figures on table to represent the general area of their firing line, although the number of figures should only relate coincidentally to the actual quantity of Boer riflemen present. The British always overestimated the number of Boers, and the Boer leaders themselves can seldom have been sure how many of their individualistic *ruiters* were in action at any time. As the Boers suffered very low casualties, from 10% at Laing's Nek to 1.5% at Majuba, it does not seem necessary to record these by removing figures, except in the unlikely event of a successful British charge.

British fire should therefore only affect Boer morale. The British certainly placed much confidence in the moral effect of their guns and rockets, and the 7pdrs at the Ingogo may have deterred the Boers from attacking Colley's layback position there. However, artillery was generally at a tactical discount at this time, as its effective range (1000-1500 yards) was not much greater than that of well aimed rifles, while rockets were only useful against area targets, which the Boers rarely presented. The Boer's coordinated fire and movement tactics were a more than adequate response to superior British heavy weapons. To reflect this a wargame should:

- allow the Boers to move and shoot, while the British do one or the other.
- require British troops to spot Boers before firing, while the Boers can always see their targets.
- check British morale *before* they fire. This would allow the Boers to pin British troops down, unable to fire.
- provide patches of ground that allow the Boers to advance unseen to decisive range.

The morale system should depend, not on casualty levels, but on the relationship between the number of figures testing morale, and the amount of incoming fire. For example, at odds greater than one-to-one the target should dice between moving or firing, at three-to-two between firing effectively or wildly, and at two-to-one between firing wildly and hiding. Numbers should be doubled, for enfilade fire, or at close range. The effect of Boer fire, from an uncertain number of marksmen could be represented by rolling one or two average dice (numbered 233445) for each group of Boers in the firing line. Their value when testing morale could be decided in a similar way, and secretly recorded in advance, under the field cornet's base, reflecting his force of personality, rather than an unknowable, and continually changing number of rifles. Only in particularly stressful situations, say one side manages to overrun the other, should there be a rout. Overruns should occur rarely, when one side is unable to fire, either through morale, as nearly happened at Schuinshoogte, or through the lie of the ground, as at Majuba.

STRATEGIC CONTEXT

Although the unfortunate results of the campaign were largely tactical in origin, the strategic context of Colley's battles is significant. He was under pressure to act before the garrisons besieged in the Transvaal surrendered. Outnumbered as he was, especially in mounted troops, he was likely to have had problems with his lines of communication even had he won at Laing's Nek. Had Colley got through the Drakensberg, Schuinshoogte might well have been fought, somewhere further down the road to Standerton, against worse odds. To taste fully the bitter flavour of the Transvaal War therefore there is much to be said for refighting its three constituent actions, in order. If the first two result in defeat, then only a historically unlikely success at Majuba will save your career. On the other hand, an early success followed by a defeat inside the Transvaal might prove as disastrous as Colley's last despairing throw did in practice.

FIELD ACTIONS

Within this sequential structure, the Transvaal War presents the opportunity for a variety of games, despite its brevity. Some may look more traditional than others, but all are very different from the usual pattern of British victories.

The most straightforward, was their initial repulse at Laing's Nek. Although the British operated on a front of some 3500 yards, the individual units took up only a fraction of this. In two ranks the 58th's 479 bayonets would require only 320 yards. If your table were five feet square, the 58th should occupy five or six inches.in line, allowing space for fifteen or thirty 15mm figures, in one or two ranks. These numbers give figure scales of one-to-thirty or one-to-fifteen respectively, the latter seeming more appropriate, given the smaller forces used later. As the firing lines at Majuba itself were greatly extended, the figures need to be mounted individually. Groups of 5mm figures on one-inch bases would be visually effective, but are difficult to use singly. Rifle ranges on this scale work out at six inches for what the manuals euphemistically described as 'decisive', that is where people get killed, even lying down, and 16 inches for extreme range where the effect is more moral than physical.

Although Laing's Nek can be played in a fairly conventional manner, British freedom of action needs to be restricted, if only to stop them rolling up the Boers' exposed left flank. This could be achieved by the crude device of deploying Boers up to the edge of the table, forcing the British into the historical frontal attack. A more satisfying approach would be for the British to decide how far to the right any turning movement should swing, before randomly determining the extent of the Boer position. Obviously, the further out the British go the less likely they are to meet opposition before gaining the high ground leading to the Boers' main position, but the more likely the turning movement is to be be delayed. For this reason, and to reflect the difficulty of marching across the veld, movement rates should be random, say the score of two dice. Depending how slowly the British attack develops, the large number of Boers beyond the British left may become restless, and attack 3/60th and Naval Brigade. This consideration may explain why Colley went for the frontal attack, instead of turning the Boer left.

The action at Schuinshoogte can be recreated as a standard meeting engagement. However, it cries out to be played as a 'Road' game. This is a solo game with one or more players where one side, in this case the British, try to cross the table against opposition whose strength and location are unknown, in order to carry out some quite unmilitary task, like bringing in some wagons. This usually results in an ambush at the most embarassing point. The British themselves initiate contact through their movement die roll. For example, if each unit moved the score of two dice, a group of Boers might appear on a score of 11 or 12, just within artillery range, either ahead or on one flank. Once met, they would spread out to envelop the British flanks, as they did, advancing through patches of long grass or dead ground. From personal observation, solo 'Road' games certainly create an appropriate level of player arrogance, until their first thrashing at the hands of the automatic enemy.

MAJUBA HILL

The final action of the campaign is also the most unusual. In many ways it resembled a siege more than a fight in the open, with its emphasis less upon the interplay of opposing forces, than upon the internal conflicts of the British. Again the need is to hinder the rational wargamer, caught in Colley's death trap.

Given the non-existent British leadership, there seems little point in assigning any game function to the senior officers present. The British players are best placed in charge of the three sides of the position, and left to compete for reinforcements from the central reserve. Although the troops originally deployed around the perimeter may be from distinct units, for example the 92nd on the north side, reinforcements should come equally from all three units present: 58th, 92nd and Naval Brigade. However, only figures belonging to the unit originally allocated to a sector should count there for morale purposes, reflecting their reluctance to follow officers from other units.

Visually, it would be attractive to build Majuba from slabs of polystyrene, with random patches of flock to indicate gullies and scrub. More practically, but less impressively, it could be drawn on brown paper, and rolled up for storage. The layout of the summit itself should include its natural strongpoints, the defenders doubling the fire effect of figures occupying MacDonald's and Hay's Kops, and Gordon's Knoll. The Boers would test morale to climb from one contour level to the next, or to move around the mountain, reflecting how they encircled the summit. The number of levels and the chance of climbing each one needs to be consistent with the five hours or so that the assault parties took to reach the ledge below the summit. Turns need to represent a significant amount of time, say half an hour, another reason why standard sets of rules with turns of only a few minutes, will not do.

So small was the British force that a further reduction in figure scale to one-to-ten, seems appropriate. Even at this ratio the summit of the mountain is only nine inches by 12, and may appear uncomfortably crowded with its three dozen defenders. With Boer riflemen all around the foot of the mountain, it soon becomes apparent how vulnerable the British were to converging fire. To reflect this, the defenders of one face of the summit should count half the fire of the Boers behind them, as well as that coming from their front.

In the early stages of the game the British must hope the fire-based morale system described earlier will prevent the Boers moving up the slopes, and collecting in dead ground, close enough to make a rush. The Boers on the other hand need to suppress British fire to allow them to advance from one patch of dead ground to another. More Boers should join in as the action progresses, perhaps each time the attack climbs another level. As losses in the British firing line mount, the British players have to decide between staying to encourage their men, or going back to request reinforcements, or even permission for a charge. Take the difference of two dice for the number of reinforcements, and make a counter-attack on rolling something wildly improbable, like twelve. When troops occupying the perimeter are pinned down, they should sneak away, one at a time, to collect along the central ridge, subsequently halving their numbers for morale tests, to reflect exhaustion and fragmentation of units. Loss of the ridge itself signals the end of the battle. As there is nowhere on the summit out of reach of the Boer fire from there, the only rational British response is immediate flight.